OUR NEW
SPIRITUAL
CHALLENGE

Books by George Bockl

Secular

George Bockl on Investment Real Estate

How Real Estate Fortunes Are Made

How to Use Leverage to Make Money in Local Real Estate

Recycling Real Estate:
The Number-One Way to Make Money in the '80s

Spiritual

God Beyond Religion

Living Beyond Success

Where Did We Come From and Where Are We Going?

OUR NEW
SPIRITUAL
CHALLENGE

A CROSS-FIRE CONVERSATION ON
TRADITIONAL RELIGIOUS VALUES AND
NEW SPIRITUAL WISDOM

GEORGE BOCKL

DeVorss Publications
Camarillo, California

Our New Spiritual Challenge
Copyright ©2004 by George Bockl

ISBN: 087516-790-X
Library of Congress Control Number: 2003113781
FIRST EDITION, 2004

Dedicated to the New-Thinking Spiritual Pioneers

DeVorss & Company, Publisher
P.O. Box 1389
Camarillo CA 93011-1389
www.devorss.com

Printed in the United States of America

TABLE OF CONTENTS

Introduction

Why I Chose the Socratic Method

The vast majority of readers will meet most of this book's new ideas for the first time. I, therefore, chose the Socratic method, wherein the reader can ask questions and receive clarifying answers as new ideas are introduced and discussed between the Sage and Everyman. Most of the new ideas are about a hundred years old, but they're still on the fringe of the world culture.

I use the Sage as a persona through whom to convey the New Universal Spiritual Thinking, and a typical Everyman to challenge its validity. For instance, the questioner asks: Why is there so much depravity and human misery on earth? The Sage answers: Spiritual evolution is only 5000 years old, barely out of the cradle compared to our human evolution, which is millions of years old. However, spiritual evolution has made some progress. The vast majority of people have evolved out of human sacrifices, witchcraft, other human fetishes, and only recently out of human slavery. But spiritual evolution is still in its infancy among millions of savages in civilized clothing – Hitler's hordes that brutally killed six million innocent Jews, and spiritless religions whose followers throughout history have been killing each other to advance their particular love of God.

The discussion deals with such questions and answers as: Why does seeking God's guidance in the privacy of our homes bring us closer to God than engaging in rite and rote and participating in noisy ceremonies? What came first, spirit or matter? Is the duality of devolution and evolution the first primal duality out of which all dualities flow? Does periodicity, the cyclical process of generation, degeneration, and regeneration provide the proof of evolution and reincarnation?

The Sage posits the difference between two eternities – the traditional one which believes in life forever in heaven after death, and a reincarnational one which believes that the soul, the permanent part of us, uses eons of earthly bodies to refine our experiences into spiritual wisdom on its endless evolutionary journey into eternity.

The Sage proposes that the only chance we have of stopping the present malevolence in our world culture is to teach the Fourth R in all our schools from kindergarten through college, in addition to the three R's of reading, writing and arithmetic. The Sage claims that the New Universal Spiritual Thinking is the next thrust of spiritual evolution, and that it will educate future generations of teachers, parents and students to view life with the transcendent idea of Wholeness. The Sage also claims that all entities in the Universe are interconnected in a cosmic Wholeness that's beyond religious Holiness, where the holiness of one religion clashes with the holiness of another.

When the Sage suggests that a Cosmic-Energy version of God is more credible than a man-image-personal God, the questioner objects...too remote, too abstract. But when the Sage explains that intelligent cosmic energy is the body of God, the ubiquitous power, the questioner remains unconvinced. When the Sage goes on to argue that cosmic energy is what illumes our minds and renews our bodies with every thought and breath we take, the questioner remains neutral, neither objecting or accepting. The answer is left to the reader.

Questions of a more practical nature are resolved by the Sage with unusual spiritual spins. Example: The Sage provides the underlying reason why there is more exhilaration in climbing than in arriving, more fulfillment in creation than in possession. The Sage agrees with Adam Smith's The Wealth of Nations argument that self-interest creates capital wealth, but the Sage adds that self-interest can also destroy it. The Sage shows how anyone can be a healer and why self-healing is the most effective health therapy.

New Thinking is the cutting edge of evolution, full of possibilities and opportunities. We dare not remain in a cocoon of old ideas just because they're comfortable and popular. There's a new kind of freedom when we crash the cocoon and become a butterfly: Life is a quest, not a tour.

OUR NEW
SPIRITUAL
CHALLENGE

Chapter One

Everyman

I'm confused about the many versions of New Age, Global Thought and New Spiritual Thinking — some are denigrated and others are highly acclaimed as the forerunner of New Universal Spirituality. You're one of the spiritual pioneers of this new thinking. I have only a smattering of knowledge of all this, and I'd like you to clarify what makes it different from the religious wisdom with which we're all familiar.

Sage

It's as different as the primitive knowledge that prevailed when religions originated thousands of years ago compared to the scientific knowledge we have today. These are some of the main differences: The New Spiritual

---

1 The terms New Age, New or Global Thought, New Thinking, New Spiritual Thinking, et al., are used interchangeably throughout the text. Generally, these designations all come under the umbrella of Universal Spirituality.

Thinking[1] is based on overwhelming evidence that the human species has been evolving for millions of years while traditional religious thinking claims it originated with Adam and Eve about 6,000 years ago. The New Thinking contrasts our millions-of-years-old physical evolution with spiritual evolution that is a mere 5,000 years old, an infant barely out of the cradle. Religious spirituality is fenced in by self-enclosed certainties, while New Thinking espouses open-ended Universal Spirituality. It is more aware of the universal law of periodicity, cycles within cycles, which opens the view to reincarnation — i.e., that our imperishable soul uses our perishable physical body, incarnation after incarnation, to refine physical experience into spiritual wisdom as our soul travels on its endless evolutionary journey into eternity. This is in contrast to the traditional belief that people who lead virtuous lives live forever in heaven in their physical bodies. New Spiritual Thinking does not deny the existence of God; on the contrary, it makes the idea of God more credible. These are just a few of the differences we'll flesh out in detail as we continue our conversation.

Everyman

I must confess, these ideas are all new to me. They're eye-opening, revolutionary. Will I be able to understand them?

2

Sage

Yes. We'll take it slowly, patiently. You ask the questions and I'll do my best to answer them simply and clearly.

Everyman

Since you emphasized evolution, my first question is: Where did we come from and where are we going?

Sage

A good basic first question. Predicated on what we now know about evolution, it is reasonable to conjecture that the human species, like myriad other species, began with a configuration of atoms that evolved into a cell, a molecule, an organism and on and on into Neanderthal man, Cro-Magnon man, and into the more complex, civilized man of today. That's the basic answer. But, obviously, there's more to it than that.

Everyman

And where are we going?

Sage

Man is on an endless evolutionary journey into eternity where his eons of incarnations become his destiny. If that's not clear, I'll make it clearer as we proceed.

Everyman

Before I question you more on where we're going, I'm still confused about where we came from. How come some of the wisest people on Earth believe in the scriptural origins of man? They've been believing this teaching for centuries, and the Creationists are furious with those who believe otherwise. Aren't they among the most moral, God-loving people?

Sage

They are intelligent, moral and wonderful people, but I question their religious wisdom, their literal belief in the biblical God and that man originated from Adam and Eve. Their views are fading as evolutionists are gaining.

Everyman

But your reincarnational ideas about where we're going are anathema to devoutly religious people. Are they misleading themselves into believing that the reward for virtue in a blissful life forever in heaven is a false hope?

Sage

I respect their virtues, but I don't agree with their forever belief. Nothing is forever except the march of evolutionary change.

Everyman

But what do I say to a Catholic friend of mine, a pillar of virtue in our city, who told me at lunch one day that his certainty of living in his present body forever in heaven is what fulfills his life with joyous excitement. "Nothing," he said, "could change my views. There are many who think differently out there, but eventually they'll all be left behind trailing in the dust of false prophets."

Sage

I'm not surprised at your friend's eloquent devotion to his beliefs, along with the millions of fine men and women who have their scriptural wisdom deeply ingrained in their psyches. It'll take many centuries before the transition is made from a biblical to an evolutionary concept of God.

Everyman

You referred to the role of the soul a few minutes ago. Can you expand on it?

Sage

The soul is more than a vague spiritual ideal. It's the permanent part of us that uses our physical bodies to gather spiritual experience on its never-ending journey into eternity. It's the monad, the chip, our permanent atom on which is writ all our past experiences and propensities. The soul is the printout of the skills and values it acquired during all past incarnations.

Everyman

Is this why we have child prodigies and those who possess extraordinary talents? Is it because these souls acquired more experience in their past incarnations? Or are they older souls who've had more time to develop their capacities?

Sage

A good question. My colleagues and I have discussed this at great length. We think it is both. Later in our conversation, I'll explain why there are young and old souls, but for the present, yes, those who made greater evolutionary effort manifest superior results in their ensuing incarnations.

Everyman

It seems that the role of the soul and reincarnation are basically intertwined, each needing the other. Would you clarify this for me, please?

Sage

If the soul is the real us, not our body, then it is logical to assume that it needs physical experience through which to evolve. Reincarnation, therefore, is more believable than living forever in one body.

Everyman

Are there other reasons to believe in reincarnation?

Sage

Yes, many. One that appeals to me most is that it's built on cosmic justice. Is it just for a two-year-old to die and not have an opportunity for a longer life in the future? Reincarnation provides the two-year-old's soul future adult experiences, while living in heaven as a two-year-old does not. Another more scientific proof of reincarnation is available in Dr. Ian Stevenson's book on children's memories of past lives. His test of 200 children between the ages of three and five (in several countries) confirmed their recalled experiences from past lives by accurately describing places and people. In the majority of cases, the children's recollections were proven to be uncannily correct when Dr. Stevenson meticulously checked the children's recalls with people who were familiar with the places and people. I'll cite other reasons as we continue our discussion, but for now let's move on to other questions.

Everyman

I've got lots of them, but one that heads the list is: Why are there so many depraved people in the world? Why is there so much human misery?

Sage

What do you think is the cause of the afflictions you describe?

Everyman

Well, we're ignorant.

Sage

Why are we ignorant?

Everyman

Because we don't know what's good for us.

Sage

Why don't we know?

Everyman

Creationists tell us because we're born with Original Sin.

Sage

Why do they believe it?

Everyman

Because they were taught to believe it.

Sage

Why did their teachers believe it?

Everyman

I give up! You tell me.

Sage

What I'm going to tell you is one of the most important ideas that has come out of the world's New Thinking.

Everyman

What is it? I'm all ears!

Sage

Listen carefully. Darwin was the first to cast a bright light on the theory of evolution. It led to religious confusion. It weakened the beliefs of traditional religionists and caused many to fall out of religion into spiritless vacuums — much worse than what they rejected. The idea that young, spiritual evolution is evolving alongside the old physical evolution is one of the most clarifying insights of our age. It provides the answer to our human afflictions and gives the basic reason for religious confusion. A bit of background: Spiritual evolution has made enormous progress since about 5,000 years ago when the prophet Isaiah, among others, uttered the first hint of spiritual wisdom, when he urged the rich to share some of their wealth with the poor. It was a fresh, spiritual idea. This whiff of New Thinking kept on evolving and expanding until we did away with human sacrifices, witchcraft, medieval superstitions, slavery and numerous other fetishes that plagued humanity for centuries.

Everyman

But what is spiritual evolution doing today?

Sage

Just as spiritual evolution has led us out of the medieval Dark Ages into the light of reason, so it is now endowing us with a burst of New Spiritual Thinking. One of its cardinal principles is Universal Spirituality, a cosmic, uniting view that will eventually reconcile the fragmented religious beliefs into sharing one another's wisdoms.

Everyman

What exactly do you mean by Universal Spirituality?

Sage

It's a challenge to old-time religions not to remain cocooned and disregard the scientific evidence of

Wholeness, that everything in the Universe is interconnected, that more goodwill is generated in inclusive Wholeness than in exclusive holiness. That's a short answer to what will be a central topic of our discussion as we flesh out the cosmic wisdom of Universal Spirituality.

Everyman

Do you really believe that religions are going to give up holiness for Wholeness?

Sage

Indirectly, it's already happening. Ecumenicism is a tiny first step. Tiny minorities are attending one another's services. Some leading Catholic and Lutheran clergy, most notably the Pope, have apologized to the Jews for persecuting them during the past centuries. Jews and gentiles are intermarrying in increasing numbers.

Everyman

I'm beginning to get a hint about what you mean by Wholeness, and I want to know more, but I want to move on and hear what you have to say about a more intriguing subject — your new version of God.

Sage

Now we're coming to an evolutionary leap that will remain up in the air for several centuries before the New-Thinking version of God lands and is accepted with the same devotion that a personal God is embraced today. Be patient, bear with me, because my answers at times may sound too new, so stop me with questions, until I make them crystal clear. But first, get set for a long explanation.

An increasing number of people are becoming aware of new insights that flow out of evolutionary science, about which the ancient prophets had not the slightest knowledge. Physical evolution, spiritual evolution, Universal Spirituality and the law of periodicity were as unknown to them as future cosmic insights, waiting to be discovered, are unknown to us today. With our evolved, new knowledge, millions are beginning to question the man-image of God, and find it more credible to view God as the Body of the Universe, One Life, within which all entities are its organs. And the lifeblood of the Universe is Cosmic Energy. It has Intentionality, Purpose and Ultimate Intelligence. It is constantly generating, degenerating and regenerating its myriad evolving entities throughout the cosmos. Cosmic Energy is as close to us as every thought and breath we take — the ubiquitous energy that keeps us and everything else in the Universe evolving. We can communicate with this Cosmic Energy God by quieting our minds during meditation and waiting for insights to enter and engage our thoughts. If we're open to God's guidance, elevating thoughts will light up our mindscape. That is God talking to us, and if we listen and act accordingly, the best in us will guide our evolutionary journey. Is there anything that puzzles you, that needs clarification?

Everyman

I can't get warmed up to your idea of a Cosmic Energy God. You're asking me to communicate with an energy. It's too abstract. It doesn't have the warmth of a personal God. You want an honest opinion, don't you?

Sage

Only complete honesty. Your reaction is understandable because the personal-God version has been ingrained in your psyche when you were conditioned during your youth.

Everyman

I'm cool to it for another reason. I'm using my business-man's logic now. Do you think the Roman barbarians could have been civilized by a Cosmic Energy God? No Way! The early Christians couldn't have done it without a personal God.

Sage

A man-image-personal God was valid for their times, but let me explain why a Cosmic Energy God is valid for our times. Spiritual evolution works with great wisdom. The uneducated Roman hordes were not evolved enough for a Cosmic Energy God. Even the prophets were not ready for this concept because they knew nothing about evolution or about the super intelligent spiritual Cosmic Energy that is guiding the Universe. The prophets did a wonderful job inspiring the heathens to give up their nihilism for a God-fulfilling life. Their wisdom has disciplined their followers for centuries, and it's still doing it today. But a new era is dawning, with new knowledge and new spiritual insights.

Everyman

Now we're getting somewhere! Show us how the new knowledge and New Spiritual Thinking are going to get us out of our degenerating world culture as successfully as the early Christians got the barbarians out of their nihilism. Let's get specific.

Chapter Two

Sage

Spiritual evolution will show us how to get out of our modern barbarism, just as it helped the early Christians to get primitive barbarism out of their heathenism. It will show the new spiritual pioneers how to view God, man and the Universe in a new light.

Everyman

I hope the new light will be shining on the rest of our discussion. But before leaving your cosmic-energy version of God, I'd like you to tell me how you made the transition from what I assume was your personal God to your Cosmic Energy God of today. Perhaps your personal experience will be more convincing than what you've been explaining so far.

Sage

It was a wrenching experience, full of guilt and fear. But after several years of discussing and reading New Thinking spiritual literature, and periods of doubt as the old and the new warred against each other, I not only relaxed in my new mindset but was newly inspired by the spiritual change. Let me describe it in detail. As soon as I sit down to meditate each morning, I feel the presence of God, when I visualize my breathing rhythms as Cosmic Energy flowing through me with every thought and breath I take. I often take it a step further by believing that the Cosmic Energy God changes some of my body's disequilibriums into natural equilibriums. And one of the most practical insights I mined during my meditations is that if I don't put anger, worry, fear and anxiety into the pipeline of my thinking, the cosmic energy flows more naturally through my mind and body, keeping me healthier and more actively alert. I feel much closer to my Cosmic Energy God than when I hurriedly attended Mass during my orthodox days. I'm now in charge of my spiritual evolution. I'm now open to new insights, no longer hemmed in by religious certainties. But I'm grateful for those Catholic certainties, because without them I would not have had the fundamental religious wisdom from which to evolve.

Everyman

How do you expect me and millions like me — who

haven't explored New Thinking the way you have — to believe the way you do?

Sage

The heathens were as uninformed and puzzled by the new Kingdom-of-God ideals as nearly all people are about New Thinking today. And just as it took centuries before the barbarians accepted and integrated religious wisdom, so it will take centuries of new evolution before people in and out of religions accept and integrate the universal wisdom of New Spiritual Thinking.

Everyman

You mean, unless we change, we'll remain twenty-first century heathens?

Sage

That's one way of describing it.

Everyman

We've covered the big picture pretty well. What I'm interested in is how New Thinking can benefit me and society now! The old-time religions have showered us with wise, practical benefits for centuries. That's why we've held onto them and won't let go. Let me pursue it a bit further. What I'm going to tell you is the foundation for all my future questions. I'm a practical man, as are millions like me who are primarily looking for benefits, now, — to fulfill our lives. How will New Thinking benefit us now? Be specific.

Sage

I'll be specific, but please follow my general reasoning. Before we got the benefits of refrigerators, we had to know the master theory of refrigeration. Most of humanity's benefits originate directly and indirectly from spiritual ideals. Let me show you in detail how New Thinking is benefiting us right now and will continue to, increasingly, in the future. New Thinking's Universal Spirituality is initiating some members of traditional religions to join interfaith conferences and attend each other's services. The benefits will be enormous and direct — diversity will flower. And people within religions will be more apt to explore the wisdom of other religions. Ethnic minorities will be spared the bigoted lash of majorities as camaraderie among diverse people replaces exclusivity. Another direct benefit to people who are probing New Thinking is a greater interest in reincarnation. For those who are losing their belief in living in heaven forever, reincarnation is offering them a new version of eternity, a promise flashing with the grandeur of adventurous incarnations as we travel on our endless journey into the Unknown.

Everyman

Reincarnation does not resonate with me, but Universal Spirituality does. Before you add other New Thinking benefits, I'd like you to describe what you mean by Universal Spirituality. I usually prefer short, direct answers, but in this case please go on for as long as you like.

Sage

Universal Spirituality will play as significant a role in future generations as the Ten Commandments did. It is not a religion; it's the essential wisdom of all religions. It transcends the exclusive beliefs of all religions. It can best be described as an unending quest for truth wherever it can be found.

Cosmic wisdom is a prize to be earned; it cannot be found in a comfortable religious haven imposed by authority. However, Universal Spirituality extends tolerance to all religions, even to the intolerant. Its goal is to remove ignorance, not to punish it.

It takes a strong will and an adventurous spirit to mine its many-faceted universal wisdom. The gates are open to the educated and uneducated, rich and poor, religious and nonreligious. Practicing the wisdom of Universal Spirituality requires something other than respectable church attendance. It calls for taking personal charge of communicating with God, rather than following a regimen prescribed by others. What raises it above the din of religious certainties is the transcendent music of metaphysical thinking. Ralph Waldo Emerson and Abraham Lincoln heard the cosmic music and embraced it in preference to the prevailing religious practices. Universal Spirituality is not for armchair dilettantes. It dares believers to test their new insights on the firing line of action. Its common-sense wisdom turns allegiances into alliances. I'd like to quote an eloquent insight by one of the New Thinking pioneers:

> "I pledge allegiance to humanity, and to the planet on which we live, one world, under God, indivisible, with peace and enlightenment for all."

Universal Spirituality is still in its infancy. It struggles to survive, like a young sapling reaching for the sun while surrounded by the shadows of older trees. But some day in the future the infant will be fully grown, and the older trees, having had their day, will fade away. Does this give you a general understanding of Universal Spirituality?

Everyman

I can see where many benefits from its wisdom will flow to future generations. But again, if you'll pardon my insistence, I'm more interested in benefits now than in those coming to future generations. Why should I rock the boat and give up my religious comfort and security for something new and hard to understand? I'm a practical man. I'll take chances in business but not in something as important as changing the religion that nurtured me. Why change for Universal Spirituality, which as eloquently as you described it, is still remote and abstract?

Chapter Three

Sage

It is not abstract and remote, but very personal because Universal Spirituality widens our view of life — we see more and comprehend more. It teaches us how to use its practical wisdom to help us get along with people. It engages us directly with the cutting edge of evolution, puts us on a quest rather than under a blanket of comfort and security. It's far more interesting to live vulnerably, open to change, than to live invulnerably in a cocoon without the fun of becoming a butterfly. Spiritual evolution dares us to be locomotives instead of cabooses.

Everyman

You have a way of jarring fixed molds. You've jarred mine about the value of security. I could challenge you on some of it but I'm so full of other bread-and-butter questions that I'll pass for now, and perhaps come back to it later.

Sage

If I've jarred you, I've partially answered your question. New ways of looking at fixed ideas are the spur to human progress.

Everyman

I wonder what New-Thinking spin you have for this one? The winning, that is the must-win syndrome in sports, business and politics has become so pervasive, that even though I see its dark side, I admit I'm part of it, sort of in the gray area. When I work hard to win in business and get excited when my favorite sport team or politician wins, I admit I join the crowd and yell, "Hooray!" Do you have a spiritual spin on this?

Sage

Whoever said that winning is everything may have been clever, but not wise. The intense winning syndrome has created more havoc than good. In sports, the clamor for winning ravages the emotions of team owners, players and fans — all the way down to many parents who drive their children to win in baseball's Little Leagues, thus instilling in them the intense-winning syndrome for life. The New Thinking is prudent about preferring winning to losing, but without the zeal that corrupts. The winning mania in sports, business and politics has such a dark side, which has become so prevailing, that the people who engage in this mania lose sight of their life's purpose, and society suffers.

But amidst the dark side of winning, a bright side is emerging. A two-year study, conducted by business professor Ian I. Mitroff, along with business consultant Elizabeth A. Denton, found that a substantial number of businesses are putting universal spirituality into the workplace ahead of intense winning. These businesses define universal spirituality as being connected with all humankind in the Universe. The investigators found that most businesses that adhere to this way of thinking enjoy more camaraderie, less labor conflict and increased profits. The spiritually oriented businesses emphasize societal contribution over zealous competition, without endangering the bottom line. They thrive on a whiff of New Spiritual Thinking.

Everyman

I've got another perplexing question that I've debated with my friends for a long time: Do institutions mold human nature or does human nature mold institutions?

Sage

A profound question. My short answer is that you can't make a good omelet out of bad eggs. Bad people will corrupt the best institutions, and good people can make bad institutions function tolerably well. Changing bad institutions for better ones does have some beneficial effect on human nature, but elevating human nature has a far greater influence in creating good institutions. We need both. But today's emphasis on secular institutions will not improve conditions until New Spiritual Thinking guides our human affairs instead of having them influenced and controlled by present institutions.

Everyman

I've never heard it explained so clearly in so short a time. I now have a personal question: Why do my creative juices flow more abundantly when I'm in the process of developing a real estate project and slow to a trickle when it is done? Other people I know take great satisfaction in possessing and keeping things, and have little interest in creating. Evaluate the differences between us.

Sage

You're more in tune with cosmic creation than those who find satisfaction in the ownership of creation. For instance, designing a chair is more fulfilling than sitting on it, composing music is more inspiring than listening to it, sculpting jewelry is more fun than wearing it. Creation is on a much higher level of spiritual evolution than possession.

Everyman

Let me try to match your picturesque examples. What you said is climbing is more exhilarating than arriving, creating more fulfilling than possessing. Isn't that in a nut-shell? But I've got another, more serious question. When I was poor, the first $5,000 I earned in selling real estate released a torrent of happiness. And now, when I earn $100,000, I get hardly a whiff of the former excitement. Apathy has replaced my former vibrancy. What's your explanation?

Sage

You need a spiritual challenge that's more stimulating than your secular challenges. You're in it now, fighting your ennui by engaging in this conversation. Don't you feel some of that same excitement as when you earned your first $5,000?

Everyman

Not yet.

Sage

Look at it this way. You were challenged to overcome poverty. Now you are challenged to overcome the apathy of arriving, after the climbing. And you're doing it right now by seeking more purposeful living. You've chosen a much better way than resorting to anti-depression pills, as millions are doing today when they don't find meaning in their lives.

Everyman

You mean I can get out of spiritual poverty the way I got out of my secular poverty?

Sage

As I said before, you're doing it right now.

Everyman

I'm beginning to feel some of the excitement you're alluding to. Although I'm still full of secular logic that asks what's the meaning of all my striving, I'm enjoying your slant on things so much that I'd rather hear more of you than bother you with more of me.

Sage

I want to give meaning and purpose to all your striving. It's the guts of our conversation. So go ahead with your questions. Perhaps we'll find answers that will directly or indirectly lead to what's bothering you.

Everyman

I'd like to switch to a less personal though important question. I have several close friends who are genuinely conservative and others who are sincerely liberal. They argue about their respective philosophies, and frankly, I alternate siding with one or the other. Clarify my ambivalence, which side is closer to Universal Spiritual Thinking?

Sage

It's an important question, one that divides most democratic countries, often with vituperative hostility. Here are the main differences: The conservative economic and political philosophy is built on three premises: The first, as set forth in Adam Smith's seventeenth-century book, *The Wealth of Nations*, stresses that the greatest spur to creating wealth is self-interest. The second holds that too much help to the unemployed and indigent turns them into dependent invalids. The third needs more explanation. Conservatives are against Big Brother or anything that smacks of socialism.

On the other hand, liberals believe that free-market economies create strong lifters and weak learners, and that it is the moral duty of the strong to help the weak. While liberals admit that self-interest creates wealth, they oppose legislation that widens the gap between rich and poor. Liberals contend that their sin in caring too much is smaller than the sin of not caring enough. This is a secular subject that has spiritual implications.

Everyman

You've given me thoughtful ammunition that I'll be tempted to use against my conservative friends. I'd like to bring up another social problem. Let me ask it from the standpoint of a frightening personal experience. Some years ago, while driving on a Los Angeles freeway, I took a wrong turn and ended up in Watts, a black ghetto. Immediately, I conjured up a scenario wherein I am surrounded by gang members. I kept on driving along streets of boarded-up stores until I came to Santa Monica Boulevard, which I knew would take me west and to my hotel. Within just ten miles of each other, people lived in two different worlds: one partially controlled by gangs; the other by Los Angeles police. What's your solution?

Sage

It's crystal clear by now that parents, churches, role models, and marginal efforts by business, while all laudatory, are not going to solve this festering social wound in America. President Franklin D. Roosevelt (FDR) stopped the formation of unemployed gangs during the Depression by creating the Civilian Conservation Corps (CCC) camps where the unemployed repaired the country's decaying public infrastructure. FDR had the foresight to do it during economic austerity, but we don't have the same vision to do it in today's prosperity. I can visualize a plan whereby the government would pay gang members the minimum wage, provide housing in barracks currently being vacated by our armed forces, plan meaningful recreational activities, and put these young men to work in reforestation projects, repairing public bridges, upgrading U.S. parks and perhaps even building homes for the poor. Socialism? No, just plain, practical economic sense for these three reasons: It would reduce crime, provide work and offer a brighter future for a 'lost' generation. Lastly, it would cut down on prison-building costs with their huge expenditures. What we have now is a national tragedy. Rather than upgrading the lives of unguided youths — and saving eventual victims — we are unwittingly and inexcusably creating young criminals. It's old economic and social thinking at its worst.

Everyman

And I think your solution is New Thinking at its best. I hope you don't mind my digressing from the spiritual to the secular.

Sage

You're not digressing. They're intertwined. New Thinking is as interested in the secular as the secular should be in the spiritual.

Everyman

Then you'll be interested in this one. It's more subtle than the gang problem. It's the new feminism. I'm curious what New Thinking has to say about the new feminism?

Sage

The feminine clamor for equal rights vis-à-vis men has both good and bad aspects. It's good in eliminating unfair practices, procuring equal rights, but it's bad in encouraging women to imitate men. The macho mindset of a husband who dominates and runs his family as owner, coach and quarterback is an anachronism that should be scrapped, especially when it shows up as the tyrannical husband who abuses his wife and their children. However, an increasing number of feminists are pushing for equal status with men by mimicking them in unnatural ways. When a woman copies man's coarse speech and aggressive mannerisms, she loses a precious part of her femininity. She violates the law of natural opposites. Feminists should work to obtain equal rights across the board, but not relinquish their womanhood.

Everyman

In this case and others, I've noticed that you always return to the basic law of nature.

Sage

That's where the wisdom of spirituality is most beautiful.

Everyman

What about the atheists and ethical humanists who find fulfillment in reason alone and who don't need nature's spiritual wisdom?

Sage

You raise a profound question. Can people lead exciting lives without exploring spirituality? Yes, they can, because we can gain raw wisdom from the grist of human experience. But that wisdom, I repeat, is raw. We need the secular input of the earthy rough and tumble, but without a spiritual transcendent dimension life eventually becomes barren and brittle, limited by finite reason.

Everyman

You emphasize the need to dovetail the secular with the spiritual, that each needs the other for a fulfilling life. I have a slew of secular puzzles, but I don't have any idea on how to connect them with the spiritual.

Sage

I'm as interested in your secular puzzles as you are in my spiritual solutions. I need the grist of your secular thinking to learn how to connect it with New Spiritual Thinking. How we meet the challenge of integrating the two will determine the pace of our collective human progress. So go ahead, begin with your "puzzlements."

Everyman

Clarify for me, please, the thin line between preference and prejudice. Am I bigoted when I prefer to live among Jews in a white neighborhood and hobnob mainly with my selected friends?

Chapter Four

Sage

You're skating on thin ice. Preference begins with tribalism when people prefer one group over another. Without basic spiritual wisdom, preferences are easily locked into tribal ethics and mores out of which flow prejudice, bigotry and violence. And on a more evolved level, religions have civilized preferences into sophisticated prejudice and bigotry. Spiritual evolution works slowly. That's why it's understandable if Jews feel more comfortable living among Jews, or if blacks prefer to live among other blacks. Most people prefer their own familiar cultures. But we're paying a high price for these tribal preferences — Northern Ireland's violence between Protestants and Catholics, the Serbs' ethnic cleansing of Albanians in Kosovo, and wars between Arabs and Israelis. What's the solution to these ingrained human proclivities?

Well, it's already happening. Secular global commercialization is breaking down barriers among cultures, religions and races. Business people are enjoying one another's diversity. But there's still a long way to go. When Universal Spirituality is taught in public schools, then preferences and prejudices will play a lesser role and diversity a stellar role. It will take the wisdom of spiritual evolution for enlightened diversity to triumph over preferences that are corrupted into prejudice, bigotry and violence.

Everyman

Now, I want to switch to a more personal problem: How can I, and millions like me, look upon our secular work with spiritual eyes? Or, to be more specific, how do I know when secular action is also spiritual action?

Sage

I want to compliment you. You're getting good at understanding the heart of New Thinking. Secular work is lit up with a spiritual aura only when we are aware that the secular and spiritual are joined. Most of us are not aware.

Everyman

How do we become aware of this?

Sage

I'm going to hold you in suspense until you describe your feelings and attitude while working on your real estate projects.

Everyman

Okay, here goes. Years ago, I moved about one thousand black families from their inner-city ghetto to nearby white residential neighborhoods. I did this by selling homes to them with $100 — $300 as a down payment. I personally signed the base mortgage, anywhere from $5,000 to $15,000. I did that because the buyers had no credit. Then I conveyed the properties to them with a first and second mortgage, but with both payments not to exceed what they would have had to pay if they rented what they were buying. My average profit was about 8% for each sale, after paying sales commissions and other administrative expenses. 95% of the homebuyers paid off the first and second mortgages in the next twenty-five years. My losses for personally collateralizing several million dollars in mortgages were negligible. It was a win/win for them and for me. Most of these properties grew 30% — 40% in value. Should I go on?

Sage

By all means. I'm exceedingly interested.

Everyman

Each of my next five ventures was the first one of its kind in my city. All were risky but profitable. I built the first modern office building forty years ago, the first elderly housing project thirty-five years ago, the first home-away-from-home hotel that rented rooms by the week or month some thirty years ago. Twenty-five years ago I converted a ninety-year-old building in the center of downtown into 110 loft apartments. I recycled a hundred-year-old building to provide low-rent space for first-time entrepreneurs twenty years ago. And there were several others that were just as risky and profitable.

Sage

Very impressive. What were your motives for getting into these risky real estate ventures?

Everyman

Profit.

Sage

What else?

Everyman

Interesting creative work.

Sage

Anything else?

Everyman

Nothing I can think of.

Sage

Well, I'm going to release you from the suspense I mentioned earlier, and illuminate one of the most profound insights in New Thinking. It's developing a feeling and a mindset to look upon secular work as sacred, to make the difficult transition from viewing the ordinary as extraordinary. When we make the change, we open ourselves to the new feeling that fuses the secular with the spiritual. Had you looked upon your real estate ventures in that way, in addition to your profit and creative joy, you would have been quickened by the inspiration that you were providing benefits to people and playing an important role in advancing human progress.

Everyman

You mean it's possible to get this quickening feeling even when you're baking a cake or fixing a car?

Sage

Yes, or running a corporation or presiding over a nation.

Everyman

But can you get this same quickening feeling working in a Las Vegas casino or making a living selling handguns?

Sage

I knew you'd get to that, and I'm glad you did. The answer is no, because deep down people shut off their still-small voice in order to free their conscience to engage in deleterious activity. Inspirational thoughts that cast a glow on work do not enter their minds as they waste their lives in secular excitement. And not until they evolve will they be able to enjoy their work with a feeling of contributive fulfillment.

Everyman

What you're saying is that if we don't care to differentiate what helps and what hurts society, and choose the latter, we shortchange our lives by shutting off a zone of happiness that comes from viewing our work with inspirational joy?

Sage

Yes, it's like settling for a life of palpitating commotion, instead of reaching for a life of spiritual serenity.

Everyman

Thank you for a whole new way of looking at my work. Can we move on to another personal question?

Sage

I'm ready.

Everyman

For some reason, as you heard me describe in my real estate ventures, I'm entranced with the notion of uncertainty. I like risk, while most of my colleagues in real estate like to play it safe. That's the security syndrome we spoke of earlier. Can you link my preference to something that's urging me to take chances?

Sage

You're one of those who is more interested in creating than in possessing, and I know why. Without realizing it, you're in tune with cosmic creation, the law of constant change, constant becoming. That you're seeking what we're talking about shows what's murmuring in your blood.

Everyman

Here's another big one. What is the difference between inner and outer freedom? I have a vague idea. Crystallize it for me.

Sage

A big one, indeed. Inner freedom comes from two sources. A conviction that we are intimately connected with spiritual Cosmic Energy — God — and a feeling that the highest good is to help others. Those who've found inner freedom can experience it even under repressive regimes, but those who are awash with outer freedom can enslave themselves in it when they don't have inner freedom. All of us want outer freedom because instinctively we don't like restraint. But we can enjoy freedom only when we discipline it with spiritual wisdom, the source of inner freedom.

Everyman

I like your two-tier answer, direct and to the point. Let's try this one, a closely related question. Is an orderly mind a prerequisite for developing inner freedom?

Sage

You've touched on one of my favorite insights. Have you read books by J. Krishnamurti? He's one of the world's most renowned revolutionary New Thinkers of the twentieth century. He died a few years ago at age ninety and left a legacy of the most penetrating, futuristic spiritual thinking. Among his many evolutionary spiritual breakthroughs was his strong emphasis on developing an orderly mind, something many theologians, philosophers and most people don't stress. Without order there's disorder, and fueled by free will, the mind has a tendency to wander off. Thus people, often unwillingly, get stuck in cul-de-sacs, quagmires and addictions. And minds that don't wander off as far, get hooked as chattering monkey minds that talk too much, or as cow minds that have nothing to talk about. An orderly mind, according to Krishnamurti, concentrates full force on the immediate task at hand without allowing stray thoughts to impede the orderly flow of thinking energy. When we understand the full practical implications of an orderly mind, our secular affairs, from managing a household to running a corporation, show visible marks of organization. An orderly mind sees more, understands more and has a better chance to find meaning and purpose for a fulfilling life.

Everyman

I never realized an orderly mind was that important. How do we develop this wonderful orderly mind?

Sage

My answer is going to be a bit lengthy because an orderly mind is the very foundation upon which to build a stable, orderly personal life, as well as a peaceful collective culture.

Everyman

Go ahead. I've emptied my mind of all stray thoughts so I can give full attention to what you believe is so tremendously important.

Chapter Five

Sage

Daily meditation is the most essential and effective means for developing an orderly mind. What organized my thinking into an orderly life was that after I came out of my daily quiet time, I immediately wrote down any unusual thoughts that were still "hot" in my mind. During the past forty years, I filled forty-seven one hundred page notebooks with secular and spiritual insights. This kept my mind honed with clarity and order, giving me opportunities to evaluate new insights, transmute some, implement others, and replace outworn ideas.

Everyman

Can you cite examples where this has worked in the lives of others?

Sage

Yes. About fifty years ago, I attended a conference on Moral Re-Armament (MRA) on Mackinac Island, Michigan. Among the thousand conferees were people from about twenty countries representing many cultures, religions and races. Their central thesis was that disordered human nature can be changed into inspired, orderly thinking by seeking God's guidance during an hour of daily meditation.

Speakers at the podium explained how daily guidance changed their lives. Their stories astounded me. A go-go girl from Sweden, in her native garb, told the audience how seeking daily guidance changed her into living a moral life she had never known before; a former Nazi storm trooper apologized for his hatred of Jews; an American labor leader admitted he had dealt crookedly and vowed to go straight for the rest of his life; a black terrorist from Kenya, after his change, joined an equally changed British army officer, and together they toured that country urging nonviolence before Kenya was given its independence; a former Italian Communist changed from what he thought was the only true revolution to what he now believed was "the final revolution" — a belief in God; a slick New York journalist who had holed up at the island's Grand Hotel with a couple bottles of Scotch to write a degrading story about the MRA, was challenged to try meditative guidance for a week. He never wrote the story. He told me in an hour-long conversation that if a "hard cookie like me" can change, anyone can.

Everyman

I'm impressed by your detailed evidence, but what puzzles me is why we haven't heard more about the inspiring power of seeking God's guidance.

Sage

For the same reason you haven't heard much about dozens of other small groups, who are practicing, with variations, the guiding wisdom of Universal Spirituality. Like Moral ReArmament, they're still on the fringes of world culture. But their numbers are growing because increasingly dissatisfied people are looking for more meaning in their lives than they now have.

Everyman

What are some of the other small groups?

Sage

Oh, groups with names like Unity, Spiritual Science, Religious Science, Science of Mind, Theosophy, New Global Thought, and others. They are beginning to form a network of universal spiritual thinking on a worldwide scale. I'm devoting half of my time from my accounting and estate-planning business to giving more visibility to these varied groups who are pioneering the new thrust of spiritual evolution.

Everyman

We've been into pretty deep stuff. How about some lighter insights that have come up during your quiet time?

Sage

Here's one — recognizing the types of people we deal with daily. The vast majority is generally divided into four categories: Those who give a lot and demand a lot — they make big waves. Those who give little and demand little — they neither add nor subtract. Those who give little and demand a lot — they're troublemakers. Finally, those who give a lot and demand little — they're the salt of the Earth.

Everyman

I know people in each category. Save a few of these lighter insights for later because my mind has just now popped with a question that I might forget asking later: Why hasn't religious wisdom advanced as fast as secular progress?

Sage

The answer will take us back into deep waters. It's easier to deal with the measurable and visible than with the Immeasurable and Invisible. There are fewer problems in probing the laws of nature than in investigating the unfathomable powers latent in man. Physical science does not ask the meaning of existence. It is content to know how matter works. Religion asks the whys and wherefores of our existence, and because thought is more ethereal than matter, it's more difficult to predict and control.

Everyman

But weren't the religious leaders wiser than the secularists who experimented with inert substance?

Sage

They were, but their task was more daunting — muting the physical urges into civilized behavior, getting the masses to agree on what is right and what is wrong, and deciding what to do with the irreconcilable beliefs in God.

Everyman

Is that why different religions were formed?

Sage

Yes, and they still cling to their original scriptural beliefs, using the powerful argument that their codified wisdom has no expiration date. They want it in its pristine, past purity. Secular science, however, has evolved from the agricultural, industrial, technological, and now from the information age, uninhibited. It has unlocked the secrets of nature with unstoppable speed, while religions chose to fight for their differences rather than advance in unity. And why shouldn't they? After all, they are promised a blissful life in heaven if they undeviatingly follow the scriptural wisdom of their respective religions, especially when it's persuasively articulated by holy wise men.

Everyman

Then what chance do we have to change all this with New Thinking?

Sage

The Kingdom of God has many doors. Religions enter them, stake out a claim, and practice their own special spiritual wisdom. The Kingdom has lots of room. Many faiths find fulfillment there, but so far they haven't learned how to get along within the Kingdom's vast domain. That's why spiritual evolution's New Thinking entered God's Kingdom. It does not ask its religious neighbors to change their faiths, but invites them to find ways to share religious diversities instead of fighting about their differences.

Everyman

But you gave me persuasive reasons why they cling to the purity of their faiths. Why would they want to share and sully them with foreign faiths?

Sage

Nothing is permanent except change. Tiny drops will eventually melt the hardest rock. Splinter groups of religions are liberalizing orthodox liturgies. Ecumenicism is becoming a popular view among fringes of old religions. Interfaith groups are springing up in many large cities. Some daring parishioners are attending each other's religious services. Time and spiritual evolution will eventually open a wide door into the Kingdom of God and allow Universal Spirituality to enter, to make its home alongside the homes of all other faiths. Its presence, within the

Kingdom, will transmute the hostilities now going on there into a camaraderie where religions will actually enjoy sharing and enriching one another's wisdom. It's far off, yes, but it will happen.

Everyman

What optimism! And what insurmountable barriers ahead, as I see it from my secular view. I discussed my smattering of knowledge of New Thinking with a devout Christian friend of mine. "George," he said, "Why should I dilute my belief in Christ with a vague Universal Spirituality, or God forbid, with the outlandish idea of a Cosmic Energy God? I'll never give up what inspires me on Earth and guarantees me a life of future bliss in heaven. Tell your guys, whoever they are, that we Christians would rather have certainty than any of the New Thinking pie-in-the-sky beliefs." That should give you a general idea of what you're up against in sharing Universal Spirituality with traditional religious faiths.

Sage

Well, you've given me a dramatic description of religion's main obstacles. Any other insurmountable barriers?

Everyman

Yes, here are the reactions I get from my secular friends who have fallen out of religion. When I try to explain the little I know about Universal Thinking, the highly intellectual ones smile benignly, as if feeling sorry for me for getting involved in such useless ideas. Others look at me with puzzled expressions, listening to something they've never heard before. And the cocky ones taunt, "You're nuts to think that people will pay any attention to what you're talking about!" So, religionists are hostile, and non-religionists are indifferent. That's the whole world. Who is left to listen to you?

Sage

The apostles of change have sprung up in many parts of the world. Keep in mind that New Thinking is the newest spiritual idea in 5,000 years of evolution. The epochal change will come from the bottom up, not from the top down, as in the past. Fewer people will believe in a sudden messianic change, while more will believe in the slow progress of evolutionary advance. We can write off our present generation, and the next and the next, but eventually future generations will practice Universal Spirituality, just as today's majorities practice religious spirituality.

Everyman

Might this not chill your optimism? New Thinking has been around, as you say, for over a hundred years. Wouldn't you say that things are far worse than they were a hundred years ago?

Chapter Six

Sage

Yes, in some ways things are a lot worse, but in other ways they're a lot better. During the past one hundred years, more people have cut or loosened their links to God and slid into the spiritless vacuum of Sodom and Gomorrah. But alongside the momentum of secular malevolence, a group of spiritual pioneers has been evolving to halt this plunge into a new Dark Age. So far, it's been a whisper against a roar. With the flood of dangerous technology, deadly weapons and increasing millions who've lost their moorings to purposeful living, the potential for a world blow-up is building. New Thinking is ringing the alarm bells and offering new universal ideas on how to avoid the looming catastrophe. The stakes are high. Success will usher in an enlightened age, while failure will bring increasing human misery.

Everyman

For the first time you threw a negative into our future. What makes it scary is that I have a lot of confidence in your insights. And what makes it even more frightening is that I agree with you.

Sage

We're both realists. Pollyannaish, divine platitudes are for spiritual dilettantes. I recall that you were enchanted with uncertainties because they were filled with possibilities and opportunities. I agree. Our future is very uncertain, and just as you tackled the uncertainties in your risky real estate ventures, with optimism, courage and hard work, so New Thinking, with a courageous spirit like that of the early Christians, is ready to do the same. Our never-ending challenge will be to clear the sludge in our culture with the solvent of New Universal Spiritual wisdom. I view it as a joint secular/spiritual venture.

Everyman

I agree, and I'd like to offer a suggestion. Might not the merging of the spiritual and secular cultures of the East and West help the spread of New Thinking?

Sage

An excellent observation. The "East is East and the West is West and never the twain shall meet" thinking is outdated. The last one hundred years have melded Eastern and Western differences to mutual advantage. We're teaching what is new in the material realm, and they're teaching us what is new in the spiritual realm. The Eastern sages have inspired us with a lot of New Spiritual Thinking, and the Western scientists have contributed more to Eastern creature comforts. The Eastern seers suggest that the West ought to slow down, while Western scientists are advising the East to speed up. Much of the New Spiritual Thinking has arisen from exchanging and sharing Eastern and Western wisdom during the past century. Together, the men and women of tomorrow, from East and West, will usher in an age of spiritual capitalism.

Everyman

Spiritual capitalism! What's that? And what's wrong with our present capitalism?

Sage

Spiritual capitalism is the next stage of economic evolution. The best New Thinking brains from East and West will be used to structure an enlightened economic system that puts people ahead of profit, but without eliminating the secular self-interest that builds materialistic wealth. What's wrong with our present capitalism is that self-interest has gone amuck. Too many large companies are using people as products to maximize profits. The speed with which huge industries are conglomerating could, conceivably, centralize them into a world cartel of benign, global, com-

mercial fascism. Their money power could control governments, small businesses and people's work choices.

Everyman

That's an excellent description of where we are heading.
How can we stop this from happening?

Sage

We can't stop it by merely changing economic laws and
political institutions. Russia tried to put people ahead of
profit, and failed, because their human nature had not
evolved out of atheism. And we will not evolve out of
greedy capitalism until the leaders of commerce come to
the stark realization that they are pauperizing their lives
when they use their self-interest only for piling up wealth,
without asking themselves, "What for?"

Future leaders of global commerce, schooled in the
universal spiritual wisdom of the Fourth R, will structure
an economy that is based on rewarding creative geniuses,
and compensating people on each one's capacities. This
economic structure will narrow the present widening gap
between the few rich and the many poor before the seeds
of social unrest grow into violence and revolution.

Everyman

You're always steering towards the idealistic stuff, but hon-
estly I enjoy your insights more about the now rather than
the ideals we'll be enjoying in the future. Am I short-sighted?

Sage

Oh no, it's natural to be more interested in the now than in the future, but the now is more fulfilling when it's also concerned with the future, especially when we believe that we can take our good karma into the next incarnation. Go ahead with a favorite now question.

Everyman

There are so many opinions about healing — from alternative medicine to more traditional approaches. There is Dr. Deepak Chopra's reliance on Eastern spiritual wisdom rather than on pills, and Dr. Andrew Weil's advice to rely on our own inner body wisdom for maximum health. Also, there is acupuncture along with a host of other healing aids less known to the public at large. Frankly, I'm confused, and so are millions of others. Can you give me a comprehensive New Thinking view on all this?

Sage

The key to self-healing is to develop a sense of gratitude for the gift of Cosmic Energy — God — that is constantly healing and renewing our minds and bodies. And the next step is crucially important. We must believe, without any doubt, that when we impede this flow of Cosmic Energy with anger, worry, fear, anxiety and other negative emotions, they accumulate and explode into all sorts of organic diseases. If we're not aware of this, and rely only on psychiatry and pills, we'll continue to build more hospitals and fill more beds with more patients who are not aware of other healing remedies.

Everyman

Do you use mind/body spiritual self-healing?

Sage

I do, but with prudent reservations. For a broken leg or any other skeletal emergency, I seek and am grateful for the expert help of the medical profession. But I do avoid medical help for most minor ills, like headaches, back-aches or colds. To keep in tune with mind/body spiritual healing, I became a vegetarian some thirty years ago for three reasons: moral, economic and health.

One: Torturing and killing animals for my eating pleasure is immoral. Two: It takes thirty-five pounds of grain and thousands of gallons of water to put one pound of meat on the table. Three: Many medical studies show that the quick-growth injected chemicals in meat are toxic and deleterious to health. Those are my physical/secular reasons for self-healing. The spiritual part begins when I stand guard at the entrance of my mind and don't allow the mental poisons of anger, fear, worry and anxiety to enter the pipeline of my thinking. And my self-healing Cosmic Energy flows most abundantly when I help people. That is self-healing at its finest.

Everyman

I'm a typical user of doctors and medicines. I tend to agree with your moral, economic and health reasons, but your spiritual self-healing prescription is too daring for me. I'll have to give it a lot of thought. My next question is a knotty one, and I wonder how you're going to untie it. Is free will a tyrant or an angel?

Sage

It is both tyrant and angel. A free will, unanchored and unguided by an ideal that most of us refer to as God, is prone to be manipulated by uncontrollable desires that lead to a wide range of tyrannies involving ourselves and others. A mind free from an ultimate attachment seeks lesser attachments. It lures the mind into all sorts of corruptions, addictions and temptations, as well as into mindlessly amassing wealth. Finally, it uses the cruel tyranny of violence to glorify power. A loose free will is potentially a wild energy like uncontrolled electricity — it kills.

That's the dark side of free will. But like knowledgeably guided electricity that provides the comforts of heat and light, free will linked to an ultimate concern becomes an evolutionary vehicle for human progress. It gives us the treasured choice to chart our own destiny. We become creative partners in tune with cosmic creation, the most precious gift known to man. With free will, we can raise our human nature to the sublime level wherein spiritual wisdom guides all of our daily decisions. Free will presents us with the opportunities to choose the pleasures, interests and ideals that glorify a life, one that flashes with the grandeur of a never-ending reincarnational eternity.

Everyman

Let's see if you can be as optimistic on this issue: What about people who yield their free will to a religion or ideology that fills their lives with flashing grandeur? Is that good or bad?

Sage

At first blush, you'd think that submitting our wills to an imposed discipline is a denial of freedom. Not so. A majority of people find fulfillment in yielding their wills to others. They find comfort, purpose and camaraderie, and they welcome the guidelines prescribed by knowledgeable leaders.

Everyman

Then there's nothing wrong with yielding our free will to some ideological or religious hierarchy?

Sage

There is. It's too high a price to pay for relaxing in one's certainty without trying to see what's beyond. It's like yielding to the comfort of dying rather than mentally fighting to stay alive when one is close to freezing to death. Comfort in certainty stifles spiritual evolution. Just as your ennui with material success brought you to this discussion, so ideological and religious certainties eventually grow stale, and their devotees do also, unless they seek new ideas to reinvigorate their lives.

Everyman

What can you say to millions who don't act on their free will, who are not even aware of it, and who show little interest in religion or ideology? Or to those who don't listen to the alarm bells you mentioned earlier? What role does free will play among these millions?

Sage

Who are these millions?

Everyman

I know a few typical ones. The forty-five-year-old maintenance man in one of my buildings leaves work every Friday afternoon, with his wife, for his twenty acres in northern Wisconsin. There he has been building a small cottage for the past two years, without any help from any craftsmen. There he hopes to vacation, and finally retire in the pristine wilderness. When he details for me the work he does on his cottage, I see a surge of joy as intense as that of my creationist friend who enthuses about his love for God. "When my wife and I spend a weekend in our unfinished little home amidst the deer, birds and an occasional bear," he told me, "I feel like the luckiest man alive!" He's completely untouched by the good and bad swirling around him. He's not interested in religion and would be less interested in what we're talking about now. He's found his ultimate ideal in his job and building his little cottage in the wilderness.

I can cite similar stories about the electricians, plumbers, painters and other craftsmen who work on my buildings. Their work, hobbies and entertainment are enough to keep them content without looking for causes or religion. Twenty-five hundred years ago Aristotle said that man was made for work. Perhaps Aristotle and the craftsmen are pointing to the most dependable source for man's happiness. And what's true for craftsmen is doubly true for millions of entrepreneurs and artists. What do you think?

Sage

You pose an interesting challenge. A person absorbed in work is least troubled by social quarrels and pays little attention to exercising his free will. He just drifts along. But from my vantage point, settling for interest in work only is not enough. Ants in an anthill also love their work. They build their tiny hills in an efficient, orderly manner. But that's all they can do. We need much more than work. Limiting our interest to work is evolutionary death. Man has evolved out of needing only bread, shelter and work. These three basics are not enough for a fulfilling life. We've evolved to a level where we need meaning and purpose, to what religions have been seeking and what spiritual evolution is urging us to pursue with New Thinking.

Everyman

I admire how you've spun free will into your New Thinking agenda. I've got another secular question that needs a spiritual spin. How does the role of the left brain differ from the role of the right brain in processing our daily experiences?

Sage

We need the left-brainers to create our creature comforts, and we need the right-brainers to probe spiritual wisdom for ways to enjoy them. For instance, you use your left brain to build real estate shelters. I use my right brain to inform people about the wisdom of Universal Spirituality. If we didn't pay attention to each other's roles, and I'd like to be a bit blunt, you'd become a busy drone and I an ineffectual spiritual dreamer.

Everyman

Before this apathy set in, I didn't need the right brain to tell me how to be fulfilled. My left brain was doing it in full measure. Like the craftsmen we talked about earlier, I found my ultimate fulfillment in the excitement of entrepreneurial work. No cause or religion came close to matching this excitement.

Sage

You've just hit on something very important. Ennui woke you up. That's why you're here, looking for something more purposeful to give meaning to your work. You may not be aware of it, but you're seeking the wisdom of your right brain to heal the imbalance of left-brain living. Do you see why you need both the left and right brain to work in unison to enjoy a balanced, meaningful life?

I've met many like you who didn't give up the excitement of success, but added what religions call God, the same God they communicate with in the meditative privacy of their homes. In this way they draw on the wisdom of their right brains to give an aura of sacredness to their love of work. They are today's New Thinking spiritual pioneers.

Everyman

You've thrown a lot of new ideas at me. Will you sum up how they relate to me personally? Why I should pay more attention to my idealistic right brain when my left brain has done so much for me?

Sage

Finding purpose in one's life is the main challenge to our right brain. How to synchronize it with the left brain so that the thrill of achievement merges with the passion for making a contribution to humanity is an ideal powerful enough to change you, and by extension, civilization. It's one of the ideals embedded in New Thinking that's as powerful as the one that changed the heathens of the Roman Empire.

Everyman

But our successful left-brainers are not like the naïve, uneducated heathens. They're educated, intelligent people not easily swayed. They are as riveted to the work they love as the creationists are riveted to the God they love. Do you really believe they will change?

Chapter Seven

Sage

You're changing right now, and so will millions of others. Here are the reasons why. New Thinking has as good a chance to succeed as did the new thinking of the early Christians. They started from scratch, but we have their wisdom to build on. They had few apostles, we have hundreds of thousands in many countries. They had prophetic wisdom, but no evolutionary science. We have their prophetic wisdom and science. Their means of communication was primitive, ours is international. Their inspiring message was local, ours is global. This is a skeleton framework of advantages that favor New Thinking.

Everyman

I'd like to focus your lofty optimism on how it has played out in your own life. Tell me which one was more difficult to change, your orthodox religious right-brain or your love of work left-brain?

Sage

First, the religious part. It was a wrenching experience to loosen my Catholic beliefs as I flirted with New Thinking. But as I delved deeper into Universal Spirituality, I realized, in the midst of my nagging doubts, that I did not have to neglect or reject the wisdom of my religious roots. On the contrary, they enriched my new ideas. I'm now free of guilt because my intuition tells me that I evolved spiritually by adding Universal Spirituality to my religious wisdom.

Clipping the wings of my go-getting left brain thirty years ago, from flying high on success and enjoying it, was far more difficult. I am the owner of an accounting firm, with a specialty in estate planning, and nothing mattered more to me than being successful. But as my religious views changed, or rather merged into universal wisdom, I became aware of a subtle insight. I could be ambitious without ambition. This was a spiritual spurt that allowed me to combine my secular work with my New Thinking in such a way that each reinforced the other. I explained the meaning of my change to my associates, and now all of us enjoy the excitement of succeeding, but always in tandem with the special feeling of universal wisdom. I've made an arrangement with my company to spend fifty percent of my time tending to my secular work, and the other fifty percent as an apostle of what we're talking about.

Everyman

How can I tell the difference between the truth that New Thinkers like you are teaching, and the divine messages of persuasive religious speakers, especially the charismatics?

Sage

A sure way to distinguish the charismatics from the New Thinkers is that the former condemn and demean others with inflamed rhetoric and paint their own certainties as the most glorious virtues. They feed on the uninformed and naïve, who become the fodder for their strident exhortations. In contrast, the voices of New Spiritual Thinking do not demean or condemn. Rather their main interest is to build bridges between diverse races, religions and cultures.

Everyman

Why are people listening more to voices that divide and less to voices that unite?

Sage

One reason is that there are more people who value exclusivity rather than inclusivity. Second, during the past one hundred years, more options and ideas have sprung up to fragment people into a Babel of new divisions.

Everyman

I appreciate your direct, logical answers. Can you be just as succinct and clear in explaining why spiritual evolution doesn't draw us more toward uniting than dividing?

Sage

During the past one hundred years, we've become so enchanted with the god of materialism that most of us have stopped listening to spiritual evolution's infant cry. Secular worship has surged so far ahead of spiritual concerns that there's almost a total disconnect.

Everyman

Let's not be so hard on the materialistic left-brainers. While the New Thinking spiritual right-brainers dawdled during the past hundred years, look at what the secular left-brainers have accomplished. We've created undreamed of materialistic marvels that raised the standard of living for hundreds of millions of people. We're enjoying creature comforts and human longevity way beyond the rudimentary comforts and short lives of the wealthiest kings of the past. Secular evolution has enriched our lives with instant communication, global transportation, labor-saving machinery, time-saving domestic appliances and a number of other conveniences way beyond anything we had in the past. And this new secular knowledge has given us many options out of which to carve and create many new and interesting careers. Perhaps the most enlightened contribution is that the commercial secularists are building pathways and bridges between nations, races and religions. Slowly but steadily, through global commercialization, we're learning about one another's cultures, and enjoying our diversity. Is it not fair to say that because of secular evolution we are truly living in a physically comfortable golden age?

Sage

We should be grateful for our material progress, but not succumb to worshipping the god of creature comforts. That's good enough for animals but not for man. We have a soul to satisfy that seeks treasures of the mind and spirit as well as comforts for the body. You say to look at what materialism has done for us. I say to look at what materialism has done to us. The unbridled god of materialism is stirring a brew of bloated creature comforts for the well-to-do, but very little for the poor, technologies that heal and kill, comforts that feed the body and malevolence that starves the soul.

Everyman

So, should we continue to dawdle while Rome is burning?

Sage

No. While divisive religions are doing little to stop our frenetic, materialistic lives, spiritual evolution is urging us to chart a new course in human history. To change our course will take as revelatory an ideal as Moses' Ten Commandments, Jesus' Kingdom of God, or Mohammed's prophetic Koran.

Everyman

Will it be as world-changing as the coming of the Messiah?

Sage

I extend my highest respect to those who genuinely believe in the coming of the Messiah. But I believe that, backed by evolution's scientific knowledge, it will take centuries of slow, inspired, incremental steps, rather than a sudden messianic change, to bring about what messianics and New Thinking are striving for. What I ask is that they respect us as we respect them. In the meantime, it will take a coalition of all religions and New Thinkers schooled in the Fourth R to heal the divisions that are fragmenting us.

Everyman

You've led me into deep waters again. I want to get back to what I deal with every day. As a starter, is the philosophy of trusting people a sound business principle? I'm curious what spiritual spin you can give to clear up the conflict between my idealism and my disappointment in trusting people.

Sage

Trusting people is a good gamble. Here's why: What you gain by clearing your mind of suspicion is far greater than what you might lose by trusting. And you can rely on the reciprocal action that the more you trust people, the more they'll trust you. Trust begets trust, and suspicion begets suspicion, whether it be in marriage, business affairs or any relationship. Trusting each other begets mutual freedom. A doubting mind produces fission, as in the splitting of the atom that produces nuclear violence. But an attitude devoid of suspicion produces fusion, as in the uniting power of atoms that produce unlimited energy. In man, fusion is the trusting power that binds relationships. Does that remove some of your ambivalence?

Everyman

Yes and no. You gave it a logical spin, which I like, but I, and most people, like to win, especially in business deals where the ideal of trust can get in the way of winning. That's why most agreements are in writing. As a practical proposition, aren't most people more interested in making money than in building trusting relationships? What can you say to these mostly-good people to convince them that winning is not the great goal they think it is?

Sage

I say that there's a dark side to winning that corrupts what is good and decent in human nature. The passion to win has driven tobacco executives to lie about the content of nicotine in cigarettes, big corporations to engage in collusion to win a bigger share of the market, and so on. And there are some politicians who vilify each other to win votes. And on an individual level, millions of relationships are soured when winning arguments become more important than respecting each other's opinions. Vince Lombardi, the fabled, memorialized coach of the Green Bay Packers, was wrong when he said that "winning is everything." He may have been a great coach, but not a wise man. When we make winning the "must" goal, it becomes pathological because then self-interest becomes the dominant drive in our lives. It destroys both winners and losers.

Everyman

Hold on! Most of the world's entrepreneurs would challenge your condemnation of self-interest. They'd side with Adam Smith, who in The Wealth of Nations laid down the fundamental capitalistic principle that self-interest is the key motivation for the creation of wealth, which in turn raises people's standard of living. To prove the validity of Adam Smith's view, they point to Karl Marx, who, in replacing self-interest with communist interest, caused an economic fiasco.

Sage

But there's a dark side to Adam Smith's economic theory. Unbridled self-interest market capitalism is dividing people into the super-rich, and the hopelessly poor who can't cope with the complex technology. Roaring self-interest is using people as pawns and reducing the power of labor to a whisper. The dark side of self-interest is conglomerating huge corporations into bigger ones, for no other reason than piling up more profits, and directly and indirectly controlling the political and economic destinies of nations, their leaders and people. The ensuing Armageddon between the collectivization of commercial power and the dwindling influence of people power has already begun: I mean the so-far innocuous marches and protests against globalizations' self-interest.

Everyman

You've certainly painted a vivid picture of the dark side of self-interest. Can you make as convincing a case for the bright side of self-interest and explain how the bright side can blot out the dark side?

Sage

A most difficult double challenge. But we're up to it, with new ideas and new solutions. Brace yourself for a flurry of New Thinking.

Everyman

I'm ready.

Chapter Eight

Sage

Self-interest must have a higher calling than Adam Smith's creation-of-wealth theory. Arrayed against the prevailing selfish self-interest of "what's in it for me," is the selfless self-interest of "what can I do for you," a giving emotion that is spreading in many communities in many countries. It takes many forms. It's a worldwide proliferation of non-profit ventures in housing, social services, health agencies and many other communal and national organizations where the founders and staffers experience a self-interest that is closer to the heart than the mind. The billions of dollars given away in charities is another kind of selfless self-interest, whereby the givers get an inspirational return of far greater value than the barren return from selfish self-interest. And a coalition of governments is expressing their humanitarian self-interest by providing billions of dollars' worth of help to developing nations through such agencies as the World Bank and the International Monetary Fund. All these things, and more, are the bright side of a self-interest, a higher level than merely creating wealth. However, as wonderful as they are, they are miniscule compared to the dark torrent of devastation that self-interest, gone amuck, is pouring down on us.

Everyman

Are you saying that only New Thinking can save civilization, that without it, our culture would collapse?

Sage

I am. Throughout history, starting with the concept of One God, new and enriching ideals renewed human progress. Only a new and more believable concept of God can save us from the increasing flood of cultural degeneration. Economic, social and political remedies are struggling to hold it back, but with little success. Only a new burst of spiritual evolution can save us.

Everyman

Tell me how the new burst of spiritual evolution is going to save us. We've talked about it in general terms, but what definite plan does New Thinking have that will halt the plunge of our cultural values? Tell me in plain language and give me your practical reasons why it will work. In the clearest chapter and verse, describe your solution, your plan.

Sage

What is needed and what I propose is a visionary, yet practical plan to reverse our degeneration with a regenerative idea which I mentioned earlier, the Fourth R. But before explaining my plan, I want to pose a question and answer. What civilized the Jews, Christians and Muslims? Answer: The stories, parables, scriptures and word-of-mouth that spread the wisdom of the prophets and apostles to the multitudes. There were no public schools to teach what was "new thinking" in those days. That's why it took centuries before educational religious wisdom was understood and accepted as a new way to live. The scriptural wisdom that has disciplined and inspired millions for centuries is no longer able to discipline and inspire an increasing new breed of sophisticated nonbelievers who are more dangerous than the barbarians of the past. Our challenge is how can we disseminate the New Thinking information among the people as successfully as the early religions did.

Here is the essence of the Fourth R plan and how to make it known to the masses: To sift and winnow the best of New Thinking and teach its universal wisdom and morality, from first grade through college, attuning the content to each age group.

This New Spiritual Thinking will have to be meticulously crafted, with a combination of old and new wisdom. The Fourth R curriculum will have to be imaginatively devised so it doesn't offend or interfere with differing religious beliefs. It will also have to placate the objections of the guardians of separation of church and state, ethical humanists and atheists. That should not be as great a challenge for us as the heathens were for the early Christians. Krishnamurti schools in India, England and Ojai, California, as well as various Montessori schools in many countries, are already teaching the essence of the Fourth R. The students they graduate are the forerunners of the men and women of tomorrow. And when the Fourth R is given equal status with reading, writing and arithmetic in public schools, we will create future generations who will bring families closer together and practice their schooled universal spiritual wisdom in their daily secular living. With the new spiritual insights, we'll elevate our human nature to seek treasures for the soul as well as creature comforts for the mind and body. The time to start is now! The solution will have to come from the bottom up, from you and me, not from the top down. Will teaching the Fourth R to present and future generations enlighten us and solve all our problems? No, but it can save us from our looming catastrophe.

Everyman

This is the most practical idea that has come out of our discussion. But the difficulties in implementing it also make it the most visionary. Do you think it's as great an idea for our times as Moses', Jesus' and Mohammed's ideals were for their times? I don't know enough to venture an opinion. It's so new, so ambitious. I'd like to get back to it later. In the meantime, I'd like to go from the future to the present. Tell me what single secular sore in our society bothers you the most? Any how would you heal it?

Sage

There are many social sores that bother me, but the sorest of them all needs a lengthy explanation. The foresight of President Franklin D. Roosevelt in establishing the Civilian Conservation Corps (CCC) camps resulted in providing meaningful employment to many idle hands during those lean Depression years. It was truly a triple win. It raised the self-esteem of the unemployed, it shored up America's public infrastructure, its neglected roads, bridges, parks, and so on, and most importantly, it reduced crime. In contrast, and to our shame and blame, today we do not offer any creative, constructive plan to salvage the lives of gang members, school dropouts or other at-risk young adults. It's ironic that while we're enjoying prosperity, we mercilessly allow our adolescents to waste away their lives. With Roosevelt-type caring, they could be rejuvenated by a modern and creative CCC idea. We could pay them a wage, house them in empty army barracks and provide recreation. Primarily though, we would employ them to shore up our deteriorating public infrastructure. To those who would call this socialism, let them come up with a better plan to solve our shameful neglect. Again, such a plan would give hope to the hopeless, to those who have no one to guide them. It would reduce crime, and it wouldn't cost us any more to employ our youth legitimately than it does warehousing them in prisons. Regardless of the cost, it would be the biggest bargain for society, and a new hold on life for the youth who desperately need our help.

Everyman

Your CCC camp idea is so logical, but apparently there is no political will or New Deal wisdom to tackle it. While you're on a roll, how about this one? Do you have any creative idea how creationists and evolutionists can find common ground?

Sage

Here's how we can find common ground. The Darwinian evolutionists pushed God aside and concentrated on random selection and survival-of-the-fittest theories. And the creationists believe in the literal translation of the scriptures. The two camps have been arguing about their differences for most of the past century. They can find common ground based on this reasoning: While the creationist God is a caring, personal God, the evolutionist Cosmic-Energy God is in fact the same God, but more believable because it is based on new scientific knowledge. Why not agree that it's the same spiritual power that guides the Universe, only differently described. Accepting this formulation does not change creationists into evolutionists, or vice versa. But it provides common ground since it does not negate the creationists' insistence on a man-image Creator nor the evolutionists' belief that God is the actual Process of Creation, guiding the Universe with intentionality, purpose and super intelligence. I tried this formulation on two of my creationist friends. One said, "We'll never dilute our view of God with evolutionism." The other, with a guilty look, responded: "I suppose we can have a friendly dialogue, if they don't blaspheme us and we don't condemn them."

Everyman

I assume that the evolutionists would be willing partners, but not the creationists?

Sage

Your assumption is correct. By now you should know why. May I turn our conversation in a new direction? I have some items that are probably not on your list. Let me turn to them, and then we'll get back to our questions and answers. Item: The rent we owe for our stay on Earth should be paid in the form of service and help to others. It's one of the ways we can justify our using the largess of the Universe. Item: If waving a wand could bring us millions of dollars and secure our needs for life, would that be a boon or a bane? Definitely a bane, because it would deprive us of the exhilarating joy of creation. The Universe is kept alive and evolving via the process of creation. Possession not originating from creation is lifeless.

Everyman

Most people would scoff at that.

Sage

True. That's because, on the surface, it defies secular reason. But if we dig deeper and compare the joy meters of those who are creatively involved with those who have inherited fortunes, we'll find that the joy meters of those who are creating register much higher than those who sit on their wealth. The reason is that one is in tune with cosmic creation and the other, with the lower level of human satisfaction.

Item: We should view our interdependence with reverence and gratitude. Developing an appreciation for and a joyous attitude in dealing with people, creates a nourishing mind that sends healing vibrations to others. I experience this double benefit when I thank the pilot while disembarking from a plane trip, when I thank the waitress in a restaurant, or praise the person who cleans my office. Or even when I write a letter to the op-ed page of the city's newspaper, praising the often maligned police for risking their lives for my safety. I get the same feeling when I praise judges who make the tough decisions to maintain law and order in my community. All these small gestures give me the wholesome feeling that I'm connected to the Universe, and the warm responses prove it. It's in our power to make the ordinary sacred.

Item: We're shortchanging our lives when we stop at reason. I'm going to give it a glancing touch because I want to save time for several other items. To rely only on reason for a fulfilling life is like sipping soup with a fork. We end up with little of life's nourishment. Reason, without a transcendent view that sees more and comprehends more, often bogs down in a useless paralysis of analysis.

Item: There's a difference between spiritual inspiration and secular joy. They vibrate on different frequencies. There is exciting joy in watching a sports event, but we experience a higher frequenced feeling while walking in silence amidst two-thousand-year-old redwood trees in Northern California. There is joy in landing a fish, a job, a trophy, but it doesn't reach as fine a pitch as when we're suffused with sublime music, inspirational literature, or a quickening insight that clarifies the purpose of our lives. Secular happiness is a vital part of living but it's enjoyed more fully when it's joined with a feeling of transcendence. Each is lessened without the other; each is enriched by the other. For a joyous, meaningful life, we need both.

Item: I'd like to introduce a bit of levity. When we're in our eighties and nineties, people tell us that we're over the hill. Well, I'm eighty-five, and I say I'm on top of the hill! From that vantage point, I can look down below and relive some of my peak joyous moments. And when I turn around, I see the heavenly blue where my soul will be going, and returning to another adventurous incarnation. From the top of the hill, I can see my past and future. It's a grand view!

Item: In contrast to this lighter subject, I want to turn to one of the most dangerous viruses that has been attacking humanity throughout history. It starts and grows undetected until it spreads its virulence into the collective mass consciousness. The evil of Nazism began in Germany with a few people — Hitler, Himmler, Goering, Goebels. Their superior-race virus wasn't exposed or opposed by enough good people. It grew and grew until it toppled those on the fence, and then sucked the reluctant "good" people into its malevolent, collective consciousness. Viruses with different names, likewise, began with just a few in Cambodia, Bosnia, Kosovo, and Rwanda, until they grew and spread into collective consciousness that slaughtered millions of innocent people. The lesson to be learned from these atrocities is to nip the viruses in the bud before they grow, fester, spread and kill. When the collective consciousness is tipped in favor of evil, it's too late!

Everyman
Does the same collective consciousness phenomenon apply when a few inspired people aim for a higher level of collective consciousness?

Chapter Nine

Sage

The same cumulative law applies to an inspired few when their aim is to build collective consciousness. But we have to be wary of false prophets with small ideas. While these ideas don't last, they do mesmerize the naïve and uninformed with destructive beliefs. The lasting spiritual ideals, like Abraham's One God, Moses' Ten Commandments, Jesus' Kingdom of God, Mohammed's love for Allah and Buddha's Eightfold Path began with one, grew with a few, and then spread to many. But because each of them had a big slice of human-nature-changing universal wisdom, each was accepted by the masses and built into collective consciousnesses that continues to this day. You should not be surprised when I tell you that the new Spiritual Thinking is one of those new world-changing evolutionary spurts. Its seeds are sprouting and growing but are still on the fringe of today's world's collective consciousness. Whether it's called New Thought, New Age, New Thinking or any other name, we must make sure that its germinal spirit of Global New Thinking is not distorted by some newfangled ideas or interpretations that diminish its epochal thrust of spiritual evolution. Our challenge today is to articulate it so clearly that it can be easily understood by the masses and integrated into a new universal collective consciousness.

Everyman

That's not going to be easy. Let's start with me. I'm one of the hundreds of millions who've either fallen out of religion or attend church only for respectability. Tell me, not in esoteric but in plain language, why I should be smitten by New Thinking the way you are? What can you promise me that is as promising of benefits as is the Kingdom of God? And how do I know what you're so persuasively describing is not the formation of a new religion or cult or one of those short-lasting ideas?

Sage

I know what you're getting at. I was once where you are and had the same questions. The most convincing answer I can give you is that if I changed, so can you, and millions like you.

Everyman

That's not convincing enough. You've been reading, studying, discussing New Thinking for many years. It's in the marrow of your bones. How can I, and millions like me, be swayed by what you say when it is so new and remote in our lives? And especially when we've become so sophisticated by reason that even if a Moses, Jesus or Mohammed came along, we'd probably meet him with skepticism. We're not like the heathens who knew little and were easily convinced when given the choice between heaven and hell.

Sage

Hold on! The heathens weren't so easily convinced. It took several centuries before the New Christian Thinking was integrated into collective thinking, before it was codified and scripturalized by inspired disciples in sacred literature. Our New Thinking is still in its infancy, clouded by vague and false versions.

Everyman

Then how do we know what's true and what's false?

Sage

We've culled and sifted much of the New Thinking during the past one hundred years. Our challenge today is to clarify it into plain universal language that is as inspiring for our time as the religious scriptures were for their time.

Everyman

I've read how the apostles, especially St. Paul, merchandized the Kingdom of God to the heathens. What is your strategy? What will you emphasize generally, and what specifically?

Sage

New Thinking will be devoid of mythology, with very little use of parables, that is, those two very powerful persuaders that worked miracles of change in the past. Our means will have to accommodate a more evolved people, built on a combination of scientific reason and a belief in a God based on people taking personal charge of seeking God's guidance in the privacy of their homes. New Thinking's immediate task is not to use inspiring scriptures — we do not have them as yet. Its task is laying the foundation for three epochal changes that are imperative for the transmutation of today's degeneration into tomorrow's regeneration. They merit repeating: Adding the Fourth R of Universal Spirituality will change selfish self-interest into selfless self-interest, and that in turn will evolve into an economic system of full world employment. Only then will future generations of teachers, students and parents possess the cosmic spiritual wisdom to heal the wounds of our present world culture.

Everyman

Now how about some specifics?

Sage

If we are to succeed, we must clarify New Thinking so its meaning and wisdom are easily understood by the masses. Let me try once more to articulate, in the simplest terms, some of the key new ideas so that you and millions like you understand them just as easily as millions understand the sublime meaning and wisdom of the religious scriptures. The difference between physical and spiritual evolution dramatically changes the certainties of traditional religions. Creationists still reject evolution's scientific proof, but the overwhelming data has established evolution as a fact, much like scientists of the past established the proof that the Earth revolves around the sun, not the other way around.

Spiritual evolution, the outgrowth of physical evolution, is a New-Thinking idea that is the most logical explanation for the cause of human suffering. As I mentioned earlier, it is only 5,000 years old, an infant barely out of its cradle. It has slowly civilized us out of human sacrifices, witchcraft, superstition and slavery. The wisdom of spiritual evolution is helping mankind to get out from living under dictators and into fledgling democracies. But we still have savages parading in civilized clothing. And religious animosities are still rife and ripping us apart. In terms of time and man's human progress, the process of spiritual evolution has barely begun.

Periodicity, an important new idea, reveals a basic law of the Universe. It is evolution's vehicle to continue the process of creation via the universal laws of generation, degeneration and regeneration. Periodicity has cycles within cycles. It provides us with the prudent conjecture of reincarnation; that is, we live, die and are born again. While the certainty that the reincarnational law applies to humans lacks scientific proof, until a new revelation appears, it is, in my view, a more believable option than living in one's body forever in heaven after death, as the creationists believe, or in oblivion, as the atheists believe.

The role of the soul is more clearly identified in New Thinking. It is more than a misty, divine wonder. It's the imperishable part of us that guides our perishable bodies through eons of reincarnations as it gathers physical experiences and refines them into spiritual wisdom. It is the soul that reincarnates, not the body. The soul is the permanent part of our life, the seed, the monad, the chip upon which is writ the distilled essence of all our past reincarnational experiences. We don't inherit a wise soul. We have to seek wisdom in many incarnations before we learn and earn the soul-wisdom that enriches our lives.

Universal Spirituality is an evolutionary outgrowth of religious wisdom. The challenge for New Thinking will be to bring back the many religious Gods that split off from Abraham's One God to a universal and inclusive One God. To repeat, it will initiate a change from a religious God to a universal spiritual God.

We believe that Wholeness is more sacred than holiness because the former unites while holiness divides, as happens when one holiness clashes with another.

New Thinking encourages us to take personal charge of our spiritual evolution. Taking personal responsibility is more difficult than relying on others, but it is always more rewarding. Most people do not make the effort to seek the guidance of God. But that ratio will change when the personal quest demonstrates its superiority over depending on others to bring us closer to God.

Seeing God as Cosmic Spiritual Energy that animates our mind and renews our body will be more difficult to explain, and harder to accept, than the other ideals of New Thinking. Even though the Cosmic-Energy God version refers to the same celestial power as the man-image God, viewing God as a person is much more persuasive than viewing God as remote Cosmic Energy. New Thinking's first step in making the Cosmic Energy God as powerful and personable as the traditional God is to point out that there is nothing that's more everywhere than Cosmic Energy. Nothing exists outside Cosmic Energy (God). Air, food, water are all Cosmic Energy renewing us with every thought and breath we take. Cosmic Energy keeps everything alive in the Universe, from a blade of grass, to a whale in the ocean, to the largest constellation, to the Universe itself. Spiritual Cosmic Energy, with its universal super intelligence, intentionality and purpose, guides the orderly process of creation.

Everyman

Your key New Thinking ideas, which you so eloquently described, are hauntingly true, but too unfamiliar for me to warm up to and not as easy for me to understand as the biblical scriptures. Your Cosmic Energy view of God is such a radical departure from what I, and the world's people believe, that asking us to believe in a Cosmic Energy God is asking too much. It's like asking us to fly when we have no wings. So far I haven't been smitten with your new ideas the way I have been with exciting real estate ventures. Tell me why my interest should be hot instead of lukewarm?

Sage

You and I have a choice: To join the huge crowd that wallows in lukewarm indifference or join the New Thinking pioneers and ride out our incarnation on a rising tide of enlightenment. We can remain stuck in cultural muck or enrich our souls with new spiritual evolution. But experiencing this new spirit doesn't come to us. We have to seek it!

Everyman

How?

Sage

The way I did: reading New-Thinking literature, attending lectures and participating in group discussions. That's what I did years ago. Nowadays you can also listen to many radio and television programs dealing with various aspects of New Thinking. Among the hundreds of books currently published by spiritual scientists, as well as by New-Thinking philosophers and theologians, I suggest *Conscious Evolution* by Barbara Marx Hubbard, *Conversations with God*, a trilogy by Neale Donald Walsch, *The Seat of the Soul* by Gary Zukav, and *How to Know God* by Deepak Chopra. I also suggest that you order a dozen monthly back issues of *The Theosophist*, a magazine that, in my view, deals most profoundly with the very essence of the coming age. To order it, write to: The Theosophical Publishing House, Adyar, Chennal 600-020, India.

Everyman

To wind up this subject, how about a quick review about what went wrong in the past that led to today's dangerous world order?

Sage

The One God idea that began with Abraham about 5,700 years ago was the first big epochal thrust of spiritual evolution that initiated man's spiritual thinking in the Middle East. Over succeeding centuries, the many-gods' influence faded in importance as the One God idea steadily gained prominence. Then the peoples' leaders made a colossal mistake by splitting their One God into many religious gods, and began fighting about which One God was the authentic One. Ironically, the many former gods didn't find reasons to fight each other. Today, millions of people, seeing the fallacy of dividing the One God into many parochial gods, are trying, with the prodding of spiritual evolution, to learn and return to the One and Only Universal God. That's where we are today. This should give you a pretty good idea what went wrong in the past and what New Thinking is trying to do for now and for the future.

Everyman

Thank you for a quick, revealing review. And now that we've covered New Thinking fairly well, I'd like to turn to the most elusive question of all: What role does death play in our lives?

Chapter Ten

Sage

Death is a cosmic gift, the gateway to another future life, filled with new opportunities for creative adventures in a new incarnation. Death is as much a gift as is life. We should view it as a welcoming, natural end to helping people and, through it, enriching our soul, the permanent part of our evolving life. Obviously, we should shun an untimely death and fully enjoy the wonders of childhood, the exuberance of adolescence, the excitement of courtship, the fulfillment of a career and the wisdom of old age. Only then should we bid a grateful "goodbye" to our body and look forward with an anticipatory "hello" to a new beginning, somewhere, sometime, in the future.

Everyman

What optimism! We should have New Thinkers like you in

hospices where patients are sadly dying without your new-beginning optimism.

Sage

Yes, New Thinking would be an enormous help to dying patients.

Everyman

You've dealt with death so optimistically, so hopefully, I wonder if you can do the same with: What happens after death?

Sage

Traditional religions offer living in heavenly bliss forever as a reward for those who have followed scriptural guidelines. In contrast, I want to give you the conjecturings of one of the most renowned sages of New Thinking, E. F. Leadbeater, considered one of the most respected clairvoyants of the twentieth century. I read his book *Life After Death*, and here is the gist of it. When we die the soul leaves the physical body and enters a life on the astral or emotional plane. There it relives the good and bad experiences of the last physical incarnation, experiencing turbulence or peace, carried over from past physical events. After some indefinite time, the astral atoms die and the soul enters the mental level of life. There the turbulences on the astral plane are mostly gone and only the peaceful ones remain.

Life on the mental plane is a period of bliss. After another indeterminate time, the soul feels the urge for more physical experiences. Its vibrations will seek sympathetic ones. For example, an evolved soul of a Gandhi, Einstein or Mozart will not incarnate as the child of some isolated primitive tribal couple. No, it will incarnate into a man and woman who have similarly evolved propensities. And a less-evolved soul will not be apt to be born into a more evolved couple. With some exceptions, these are the general assumptions. Despite Leadbeater's renowned spiritual clairvoyant reputation, along with those who hold his views, I would not want to offer it to you as fact, only as a speculation held by some spiritual clairvoyants who have devoted lifetimes of study to this mystery.

Everyman

Of all your new ideas, this is the newest and the most esoteric, the most mystifying. I've never heard it explained this way before. But while I'm digesting my doubts about this speculation, how about telling me how New Thinking can benefit me in life after death and in my present incarnation, and increase my chances for a good life in the next incarnation?

Sage

I'll try to answer your three questions in the order you asked them. In our present incarnation, the spiritual wisdom of New Thinking widens and refines our relationships to God, man and the Universe by filling in the gaps left by traditional religions. The scriptures say nothing about man's evolutionary journey that has lasted millions of years; nothing about Wholeness, the concept that all entities within the Universe are interconnected in One Universal Life; nothing about spiritual Cosmic Energy, which is both Creator and creation; nothing about the cosmic law of periodicity that generates, degenerates and regenerates all entities within the Universe. The writers of religious scripture were unaware how their wisdom could pit one religion against another. The forthcoming thrust of spiritual evolution will not only fill the gaps, but will also give us a more comprehensive, more credible view of God and a better understanding of the difference between the more evolved and the less evolved souls we deal with daily on Earth. Those, and others, are valuable benefits.

Secondly, we can conjecture, based on E. F. Leadbeater's clairvoyant perception, that by leading a New Thinking life, we'll have less turbulence and more peace in life after death.

And thirdly, the skills and wisdom we gather in the present incarnation, we'll inherit in the next. New Thinking will enrich future lives.

Everyman

These new insights, I admit, can help us become more worldly, more interesting people, and according to you, spiritually wiser. Can I press you a bit further? Will you cite a specific insight that changed you in a big way?

Sage

Yes. The difference between religiously imposed discipline and self-imposed discipline. My parochial discipline was seeded subliminally with strong preference, and often prejudice, while my present self-imposed discipline opens more doors to freedom and new spiritual wisdom.

Everyman

Are you saying you were a bigot at one time?

Sage

No, that's stretching it too far. But I was only comfortable in my own religion, and with my own small group of ethnic friends. Other people and ideas not only did not interest me, they seemed strange. While I may not have been a bigot as such, I nevertheless lived in a sophisticated form of tribalism. When New Thinking opened my eyes to the concept of Wholeness in the Universe, to people of other religions, races and cultures, then yes, the change was drastic and dramatic.

Everyman

Have you encountered in your readings of New Thinking literature anything that is as sublime as some of the biblical scriptures?

Sage

Indeed I have, and I carry it with me. It's a beautiful pas-
sage by G. A. Farthing, a prominent Englishman and a New
Thinking spiritual pioneer:

From the depths of the dark, muddy waters of materialism, a great spiritual universal force is rising, the first gen-
tle human rustling that is passing over and parting the
dark waters. The parting is inspiring people to discover
new spiritual treasures. This spirit is a force that can neither be hindered or stopped. Those who recognize it and
feel that this is the supreme moment of their salvation will
be lifted by it and carried beyond the illusions in our
midst. The joy they will experience will be so poignant and
intense, a bliss which will be a foretaste of the knowledge
of the gods, the knowledge of good and evil, and the fruits
of the tree of life.

Everyman

Here's a question as big as God. I wonder how you're
going to answer it in a few sentences. Will God's identity
elude us forever? Will we ever know who or what is God?

Sage

Let me begin with this most undeniable fact: The eternal
search for God's identity will continue as long as evolution
endures, and that's forever. Mankind went from believing
in many gods, to One God, then to codifying God, and now
to New Thinking Cosmic Energy God, which is an attempt

to make God more believable, not more identifiable. Who and what is God will continue to elude us forever, because this knowledge lies at the core of the cosmic wisdom of evolutionary creation, which will go on forever. The constant becoming will never cease, and the good tidings for mankind are that since our souls are part of the Universe, so we too will be in a constant evolutionary state of reincarnational becoming. Does that answer your question?

Everyman

I don't know enough to dispute it. But I've got another one that's just as elusive.

Sage

Go ahead, I'm ready.

Everyman

What should be the ultimate purpose of man? I've heard and read many different answers, but you have a way of getting directly to the heart of things. So I'm expecting something unusual, something I've never heard or read before.

Sage

I'll try not to disappoint you. Philosophers, theologians, religious pundits and mystics have all pondered this question for ages. We're still in a fog about our main purpose. Religions have their purpose, ideologues fight for their causes, and materialistic people have no higher purpose than their own self-interest. Hence, we're saddled with a Babel of purposes, some good, some bad. Framing the main purpose for my life was difficult in the midst of all those options. The combination of New Thinking insights I've mined during meditation and seeking God's guidance eventually crystallized my main purpose in life based on this reasoning: Since nothing fulfills me more than helping people, I concluded that should be the primary purpose of my life. It was a win/win purpose, for me and for humanity. That's as clear and uncomplicated as I can make it. Thus, the primary purpose of my life is finding ways to help people. All else is secondary detail.

Everyman

You made it quite clear. It's a win/win for the helper and the helped.

Sage

You've got it. But you must practice it to actualize its benefits.

Everyman

While you're in a clarifying mode, perhaps this is a good time to ask you to clarify further what we discussed earlier regarding how to build bridges between creationists and evolutionists. Your earlier explanation didn't quite satisfy me.

Sage

Creationists are wonderful people. I admire them for their high moral standards and genuine love of God. But because they are so inspirationally fulfilled with their man-image scriptural God, they refuse to have it sullied by evolutionary claims. But the differences shouldn't prevent us from honoring each other's beliefs, especially since neither can prove beyond doubt what each believes.

Since both views can't be proven, why not build bridges of friendly dialogue instead of walls of certainties that lead to hostilities? Why not create an appeal to creationists and evolutionists whereby a person Creator and the evolutionary process of creation are one and the same God, but with different designations? Why not agree that respecting each others' interpretations is spiritually wiser than to claim, "We're right and you're wrong."

Everyman

Because your ideas are so new to me, filling the gaps of previous explanations is helpful. Can I return again to reincarnation? You've already given me some illuminating information, but I want to know more. It's so intriguing and so new to me.

Sage

Reincarnation is such a logically promising road to eternity, yet so few in the West are seeking more information about a future leading to eons of adventurous lives. I'm glad you are. In my view, this is the most clinching argument in favor of reincarnation. If we assume there is justice in the cosmos, then where is the justice when a one-year-old child dies and is therefore precluded from enjoying a mature life in heaven, using the creationist's mode of belief. But there is justice in reincarnation because that child's soul would leave the infant body and be reincarnated in a future life. Thus, that child's soul could conceivably live to a ripe old age in a new body, and continue incarnating in endless future lives.

Everyman

Are there other reasons just as convincing?

Sage

Yes. The intuitive wisdom of prophets, the grand perceptions of an Einstein, a Gandhi or a Goethe could not have evolved in one lifetime. A more reasonable explanation is that their unusual capabilities were the accumulation of extraordinary insights that were forged during past lifetimes. How can we explain how child prodigies effortlessly master higher mathematics or difficult musical scores, while others, exposed to the same opportunities, can't learn them in an entire lifetime? It would be the height of pessimistic and unscientific reasoning to believe that where we are is the end of our evolution. Whether we feel the validity of reincarnation intuitively or accept it on the basis of logical conjecturing, it charges our lives with a vibrancy that only a belief in future lifetimes can bring. Reincarnation is believed by millions of Hindus and Buddhists. It is also a prudent conjecture among well-known Western thinkers, such as Ralph Waldo Emerson, Benjamin Franklin, Thomas Edison and many others.

Everyman

These are all convincing reasons. Why then didn't the Western religions integrate reincarnation into their faiths?

Sage

A good question. I hope I can give you as good an answer. It's prudent to conjecture that the hierarchies of various religions believed that a personal God of reward and punishment would be more persuasive in controlling and converting the uneducated masses. It worked. The Hebrew, Christian and Moslem anthropomorphic God not only disciplined their followers but also elevated their human natures to higher standards of morality. The personal, man-image God progressively shaped three great religious civilizations. Today's New Spiritual Thinking would not have a spiritual foundation on which to build without their contributions.

Everyman

Why then didn't the Hindus, Buddhists and others choose the same man-image personal path to God?

Chapter Eleven

Sage

About 7,000 years ago, a few visionaries at the foot of the Himalayan Mountains began speculating about ways to inspire people to perfect their human natures. That's when the Hindu religion was born. The values and virtues taught then were strikingly similar to the values and virtues that the sages of the West, beginning with Abraham, were urging the desert nomads of the Middle East to contemplate in the spirit of One God. But because of the snow-capped Himalayans that pierced the sky, whose immensity must have awed the Eastern sages, they chose to express God in terms of Wholeness, that is, the principle that everything in the Universe interconnected. And Buddhism, which grew out of Hinduism, emphasized the perfectibility of man through the Eightfold Path rather than appealing to a personal God. It was a prescription of values as vital to Buddhists as the Ten Commandments were to the Hebrews.

However, the yearning for a life after death was as natural a human urge in the East as it was in the West. So the Eastern seers conceived the theory of reincarnation. It opened the gates of eternity to them, as did the promise of eternal life in heaven to those believers in the West. After all, they were closer to the cyclical forces of nature than were the desert prophets of the Middle East. Hence, their predilection for cyclical perpetuity or reincarnation. We therefore have two versions of eternity. One that aspires to constant spiritual growth through evolutionary cycles, and the other that holds we live on forever in heaven.

Everyman

I heard a lecture on the radio wherein a scientist was saying, that according to cosmological data, the Earth is four-and-one-half billion years old and that it has another four-and-one-half billion years to live. If that is correct, then both the creationists' eternity and that of the reincarnationalists will come to an end. But by definition, eternity never ends. Are we misusing the meaning of eternity? What's your explanation?

Sage

Our souls, and this is a prudent conjecture, may continue to evolve on another planet after the Earth can no longer

116

support life, and either disintegrates or is reformed to another universal entity. I know this is farfetched speculation, but two prominent clairvoyants, E. F. Leadbeater, referred to earlier, and Annie Besant, an English seer, wrote a book titled *The Hidden Side of Things.* In it, they claim that man existed on the moon until it could no longer support life, and then those moon souls migrated and continued to evolve on Earth. I don't expect you to believe this, nor do I expect you to believe that hundreds of thousands of years ago, a continent known as Atlantis, with an advanced civilization, sank into the Atlantic Ocean when the earth had one of its rare cataclysmic tremors.

Everyman

Before we go on, I have a suggestion. I'm famished and you must be just as hungry. Why don't you take a rest while I prepare two vegetable sandwiches and a couple of glasses of cranberry juice? Eating will give us vigor to continue.

Sage

The half-hour of rest and the Cosmic Energy of your food renewed my body and triggered my mind to turn the tables and ask you a question: Why do we need a belief in God to guide our evolution?

Everyman

I've never given it any thought so I wouldn't know where to begin.

Sage

But your life is so deeply involved in it. Shouldn't you have some idea?

Everyman

I'm embarrassed to tell you, but I don't. And I'm doubly curious now how you're going to answer your own question.

Sage

Voltaire said: "If God did not exist, it would be necessary to invent Him." That's an existential quip that really throws little light on the existence of God. But there's no doubt about the existence of the Universe. And since God is the Universe, the Cosmic Energy that guides everything within the Universe, then God guides us, as well. But because we have free will, many choose a means of guidance other than seeking it directly from God, such as reading religious scripture, listening to clergy and participating in various ceremonies. All are helpful, but fall short when compared to the guidance we receive during daily quiet time when we seek it directly from God. Listening for guidance during meditation brings me closer to God than when I rushed to church to hear Mass, the way I used to before I met New Thinking. Those who spurn the idea of needing any help from God are really turning their backs on the obvious source of their existence.

Everyman

That's logical and therefore very persuasive. But let's return to the questions. I've got one I think I know the answer to, but I'm curious about the extra spin you might give it. How would finding life on other planets change religion's view of God?

Sage

Creationists would have to rethink their religious certainties and investigate the credibility of evolution's spiritual wisdom about the nature of God. Finding life on other planets would stretch people's imagination to think universally as well as earthly. If we find new planetary forms of life — or if new forms discover us — our religious thinking will take a giant leap forward. That's when Universal Spirituality would be speeded up to move from the fringe into the mainstream.

Everyman

I want to turn again to why you're so high on seeking God's guidance during meditation. If doing that is so wonderful, why don't more people practice it?

Sage

The answer lies in the need of human nature to share holy experiences with like-minded people. It's a natural, wholesome urge. The camaraderie found in church attendance, the singing of hymns, listening to sermons and celebrating holidays is less arduous and much more fun than seeking God's guidance in the privacy of our homes. Actively seeking God's guidance enriches the soul with a higher order of fulfillment. The change from relying on the authority of others versus the challenge of taking personal charge of getting to know God, requires more self-discipline than church attendance. How we traditionally approach God is so deeply ingrained in the world culture that only a fringe few, who are more serious about knowing God, are willing to change from the comfort of the old way to the greater effort of the personal way. Another reason people cling to the traditional way is that it has done so much good. But today's good is not good enough. To halt the world's cultural degeneration, we need more men and women who seek God's guidance in the privacy of their homes

Everyman

But it's human nature to prefer comfort to effort, when religion offers so much and asks so little. Why change from pleasant church attendance, to setting aside an hour a day out of a busy schedule in order to seek God alone at home rather than with the camaraderie of parishioner-friends?

Sage

I grant you the difficulty. But please grant me the fact that mere church attendance, though laudable, is not inspiring people to make the drastic changes the world so desperately needs. The easy, comfortable way is obviously not enough. What I was doing was hardly enough during my Catholic days when I feather-touched God with my intermittent church attendance. It wasn't until I met New Spiritual Thinking and began seeking God's guidance at home, in addition to attending church occasionally with friends, that God began to play a greater, more vital role in my life.

Everyman

I have another question. What role has mythology played in man's rocky relationship with God?

Sage

That's an important question; I commend you for asking it. Religion and mythology are inescapably intertwined. Before religion was codified, African tribal leaders used mythological stories to explain and to persuade their followers to identify what was good and what was bad. They urged the people to express their yearning for good, which they viewed as God, and warned them to reject the bad, the anti-God. They concocted the most bizarre mythological tales to illustrate the difference between good and bad, from which they gleaned values to guide their lives.

Later, Christian missionaries arrived with their biblical stories. As a result, many African tribes were converted to Christianity. All their earlier primitive myths were replaced with more believable stories about the eternal search for meaning. You see, spiritual evolution using mythology was able to satisfy humanity's hunger for meaning. This use of myth went on for centuries. But now science, along with New Spiritual Thinking, is questioning the role of religious mythology.

One of the most daring examples of it is *The Book of J*, written by Yale University professor of literature Harold Bloom, along with David Rosenberg, an authority on pre-Christian Hebrew hieroglyphics. The authors claim that the stories in the five books of Moses were written by a gifted story-telling woman during the time of King Solomon. They claim that these historic/religious characters were so believably portrayed that the Jews converted the stories into a religion. The rabbinate, of course, discarded this as a lot of hogwash.

Nevertheless, this claim points out the powerful impact that stories play in shaping cultures. Gripping stories spread and when they're imaginatively told, many are accepted as truth. Spiritual evolution has used mythological means with great success. However, with the advent of modern science, myths are losing much of their persuasive power. The world is in dire need now of a new macrocosmic story that combines three elements: Ancient religious wisdom, modern science and the original Universal One God, before God was fragmented by religion.

Everyman

A Universal One God seems to be one of the centerpieces of your thinking.

Sage

Well, it is, and for good reason. Look at it this way. When the story of Universal spirituality is persuasively told, then religious wisdom and evolutionary science will join to blaze a new trail, to the One Universal God.

Everyman

Wait a minute! I thought science is the enemy of religion.

Sage

I'm not talking about scientists who are only interested in a mechanistic Universe. I'm referring to spiritual scientists who regard science as wonder, and spirituality as wisdom. After years of exploring the limitless laws of nature, Albert Einstein and other famous scientists moved from wonder to cosmic spiritual wisdom. They proclaimed that their noblest motive for continuing scientific research was to explore inner man as well as the outer Universe.

For secular scientists, the search for coherent laws ends in equations. For the spiritual scientist, equations are not enough. Their quest for material knowledge is bound up with what it will do to enrich the soul, to mesh the microcosm with the macrocosm, to link the observer with the observed. Einstein summed it up best when he said, "Religion without science is blind and science without religion is lame." Because scientists are as pivotal for our times as the prophets were for their times, it is essential that scientists fuse wonder with wisdom. Their doing so will help us today as the prophets helped people in the past.

Everyman

I notice you don't ever refer to supernaturalism, psychism, mediumship or any of the paranormal phenomena. Why not?

Sage

Because those are the sensational barnacles that give New Thinking a bad name, a distorted evaluation. Spiritism diminishes the word "spirit" and has nothing to do with genuine essence of New Thinking. After rejecting mythological miracles, we would be less than prudent to fall into the trap of accepting supernatural "miracles," which border on entertainment and sensationalism.

Everyman

Can we turn now to something we touched on earlier? It's so important to me that I'd like to get another slant on it. What is the main purpose of our life? Before you tell me, here is what my friends told me when I posed this question to them, "Live to the hilt, you live only once." "Take care of my family." "Never gave it a thought." "Enjoy my work." "Be a good person." "That's for philosophers, not for me!" These views, it seems to me, are typical of the vast majority. What additional thoughts do you have on this most important question?

Sage

It is one of those ultimate questions. I've wrestled with it for many hours during many meditations. I've read the opinions of philosophers and theologians but they didn't satisfy me. Creationists would probably say that worshipping God was the ultimate purpose for them. They are looking for personal salvation, for the reward of living in heaven forever. Even reincarnationalists are doing good work in the hope of creating good karma for the next incarnation. In each case they are looking for a reward, for a return on their good works. What is it then, I asked myself, that asks for no return, no reward?

One morning an insight came to me that went something like this: I stretched my imagination to visualize what kind of civilization we would have if the ultimate purpose of man was to help others. The more I thought about it, the clearer it became. I reasoned that this is what Jesus must have meant when he told his followers that the main purpose of mankind is to love one another, to help one another. After much meditation, I came to the conclusion that helping people was going to be my ultimate purpose in life and that I would use whatever creative ability I possessed to find ways where I could be most helpful. It's a simple yet profound insight that embraces all life.

Everyman

It's surprisingly simple, yet so profound when you come to the conclusion that Jesus' teaching to love one another in its practical human essence simply means to help one another. That's so logical, why didn't religions think of it?

Sage

Because they were more interested in personal salvation than in helping people.

Everyman

You're saying that helping people, without looking for a reward or return, is a more ultimate purpose than loving God for personal salvation?

Sage

I do believe that. I climbed many steep steps before coming to that conclusion.

Everyman

So far, my questions haven't stumped you. I wonder if this one will. Why is it so difficult for people of different religions to share and appreciate each other's beliefs?

Sage

Because there is no stronger emotion than devotion to God. And when that emotion is made holy by charismatic leaders, devotees can be fired up to give a life or take a life for the love of God. The Christian Inquisition and the Moslem Holy Wars are prime examples. The sharp divisions result more from the educated leaders than they do from the less-knowledgeable followers. The clergy exhort their flock to love God, but many of them stir up animosities against those who love God differently. It's ironic that the most orthodox of each religion are often the most vehement in blaspheming rather than loving one another. When hostility becomes deeply ingrained in a religion, it becomes a persecutorial addiction, and a powerful evolutionary idea is needed before people will loosen their grip on the old and embrace the new.

Everyman

This is the first time I've heard you speak so negatively about old-time religions.

Sage

I'm not against religions, but rather I am against clergy who have steadfastly missed opportunities to direct their wisdom toward joining with other religions to enrich lives. Instead, they have exhorted their followers to diminish lives.

Everyman

Then what chance is there for the three great Western religions to share their wisdom with others?

Chapter Twelve

Sage

What chance did the few early Christians have of converting the barbarians of the Roman Empire to a belief in the Kingdom of God? Next to impossible. Yet it happened because the critical mass of debauchery and conquest exploded and spiritual evolution was there with New Christian Thinking to pick up the pieces. After four centuries of spiritual pioneering, the Kingdom-of-God ideal initiated a new civilized age of enlightenment. New Thinking, or let's call it Universal Thinking, has a much easier task. It does not threaten traditionalists with a new religion; it only wants them to accept Universal spirituality as additional wisdom for building bridges among religions. Religious people are needed to defuse the minefields between warring God-loving peoples. By joining with New Thinking pioneers they can together usher in a new age of enlightenment for our times, just as the Christians did for their times.

Everyman

I know a few creationists, as well as many traditionalists, who will never change. It's like asking them to die. They brand Universal Thinking as just another cult.

Sage

Let me give you a compelling reason why they'll change. The quest for new spiritual ideas is now coming from the bottom up, not from the top down. It's a grassroots search. Today's flocks are no longer sheep obeying hierarchical shepherds. They're not only questioning clergy, but blaming them for their inability to avoid conflicts that kill millions.

They question the clergy's ability to halt our plummeting moral values. In sum, they call for a spiritual transformation that will give the grassroots people something new and inspiring and real to live for. These are the people who are more aware of the immoralities and abnormalities in their midst, than those at the top, who are barely in touch with the decadence below. Universal Thinking is a peaceful revolt from the old traditional ways that have had their day. It is a new approach to heal our wounded culture. Hundreds of thousands of universal spiritual pioneers, the apostles of peaceful change, are ready, as were the early Christians, to make the impossible possible.

Everyman

While we're in this serious mood, I'd like you to untangle a conundrum that has me puzzled. Which came first, spirit or matter? I've read an article by a scientist who claimed that spirit, that is, life, evolved out of matter. The author concluded that after the Big Bang, fiery energy cooled and formed new constellations and planets, such as Earth. Matter, water and air then combined into a "soup," where low-level life oozed out of the muck and evolved over millions of years into different species, including man. In the process of expanding life, man's consciousness also evolved and gave life exalted names, such as Spirit, Divine Mind, Jehovah, Allah and God. What do you think about the author's reasoning?

Sage

Let me begin with a bit of background. Spirit, Cosmic Energy, Universal Consciousness, Divine Mind, God, are all synonymous. Spirit is the primary, ubiquitous energy of the Universe. Matter is the densification of this primary spirit. Matter is the devolutionary densification of spirit. Devolution is the opposite of evolution, where spirit descends into lower grade energy — matter — and then matter evolves back to its Spiritual Source whence it came. Devolution / evolution is the primal duality from which all other dualities flow. There is no lifeless matter in the Universe. Everything from the densest mineral to the most evolved sage is vivified by spiritual energy. Only the level of consciousness differs. There is no spiritless matter; spirit is all in all.

Everyman

I was in deep water when I asked the question; now I'm over my head! I've never heard this before. It's all so new. With the little I know, I choose your explanation over that of the scientist. This is indeed transcendent stuff, very interesting. My friends wouldn't have the slightest idea what we're talking about. Yet it is so basic to where we came from and where we're going. Why then don't we know more about it?

Sage

Because our five senses confront our consciousness with the visible here and now, and we have to respond to it. Meanwhile, the invisible leaves us alone and has to be discovered by introspection before it spiritually lights up our minds. That's why most of us find happiness mainly in pleasing our five senses.

Everyman

Do you believe New Thinking can increase our interest in the invisible and play an important role in our lives?

Sage

As a result of my introspection in New Universal Thinking, my relationship with God has undergone a colossal change. It has become as personal and intimate as is the creationist's relationship with God, even though we approach God from different directions. How is that possible? That's the story of my life, and the story of my initiation into New Spiritual Thinking.

Many years ago, after a successful career in accounting and estate planning, success lost its salt, as in your case, and an ennui set in that robbed me of my usual secular vigor. I began to question the meaning of sufficiency of success. I attended church apathetically; it, too, had lost its salt. Scriptural wisdom turned to repetitive platitudes. I was treading water and making no headway in my secular and religious life.

Then I encountered two new ideas that relieved my business doldrums and religious atrophy. It was Moral ReArmament (MRA), which we discussed earlier, that raised my consciousness to finding common ground for all religions, races and cultures. The other idea was seeking God's guidance during an hour of quiet time each day in the privacy of my home. After attending a dozen conferences and meetings on Mackinac Island and later visiting MRA's world headquarters in Caux, Switzerland, I was a changed man. The first idea introduced me to the difference between religious wisdom and Universal

Spirituality. The second opened a new and personal path to God that I had never taken before. Both ideas widened the view of my experience. They changed dandelions to roses.

And that was just the beginning. A few years later, one of my associates put a magazine on my desk and said, "Read this! It's right up your alley." It was the magazine, *Theosophist*, I mentioned earlier. That was the beginning of a forty-year universal spiritual education. It introduced me to the past one hundred years of New Thinking. It opened doors to views about God, man and the Universe that had been completely closed to me, and I can safely say, new to the vast majority of people on Earth.

For instance, how many people do you know in or out of religion, who have any cogent ideas about the vital difference between Universal and religious spirituality? And if you were to ask people. "What is the main cause of human misery?" the chances are that none would attribute it to the fact that spiritual evolution is only about 5,000 years old, while physical evolution is hundreds of millions of years old. And those seeking God's guidance during meditation are a miniscule few compared to the vast numbers of parishioners who are satisfied with occasional church attendance.

How many people realize that religious leaders made a big mistake when they fragmented Abraham's One God into many religious Gods, a blunder that resulted in the killing of millions of innocent people? Very, very few. How many people do you know who are aware that New Universal Thinking is trying to bring back the idea of the Original One Universal God? These and other new ideas have made an enormous change in my life. They vivified my business doldrums and woke up my onetime religious apathy with a burst of spiritual evolution. Shall I go on?

Everyman

Please do. I like it when I see a light in your eyes.

Sage

The law of periodicity, cycles within cycles, clarified for me the meaning of birth, death and rebirth in a way that nudged me closer to the belief in reincarnation, the law I see operating in nature. This reasoning led me to believe that the soul, my imperishable seed, is what incarnates me into eternity.

But my New Thinking does not stop at these life-defining ideals. I'm a practical businessman like you are. New Thinking is inert unless it leads to action. Nothing happens until we test our big-picture ideas in little daily events. That's why I'm working with others to get the Fourth R taught in public schools. In my view, it's the only way to educate future generations to stop trampling on our freedoms and taming our wild, selfish self-interest that is corrupting democracy.

You see a light in my eyes. What you don't see is the Cosmic Energy, God, that is flowing through my mind and body, renewing my body and illuminating my mind as I speak.

Everyman

My interest in New Thinking rises when you speak from personal experience. I've now come closer to knowing you as a person as well as a sage. This new feeling has pumped up my courage to digress for a moment, and ask your personal advice about what to tell my two teenagers, a boy and a girl, that will help them to avoid the sexual peer pressures of their friends. What would you say to my wife and me to help us put our children on a course leading to a more meaningful life?

Sage

What do you do before you recycle an old building to a new use? What do you check out before you have a clear picture of what lies ahead?

Everyman

The most important checkpoints are location, the cost of construction, potential gross rent, and cash flow after operating expenses and debt service. And when I work hard and fuse all these elements in an orderly manner, then I stand a good chance of producing a profitable real estate venture. What's your reason for asking this?

Sage

Tell your teenagers in a two-way, leisurely discussion that

life is a wonderful adventure, and the more you prepare for it, the better chance you'll have to enjoy it. Describe in clear detail the challenges — the checkpoints — that lie ahead and how to handle them.

Checkpoint Number One: Discipline the youthful sex drive. Tell them that anticipation and courtship can be just as exciting as consummation and that the reward of waiting until the right life-mate comes along is an assurance of having a healthy body.

Checkpoint Number Two: Find a mate with whom to develop a binding love based on what each can give to the other, and not settle for what each can get from the other. When this reciprocal-giving feeling is mutual, the disciplined anticipation and courtship will be worth all the waiting.

Checkpoint Number Three: Tell them that it's very important to choose a profession, craft, service or any other work that makes a positive contribution to society. Caution them to avoid the quick buck or any occupation that in any way hurts society.

Checkpoint Number Four: Raise a family. Tell them that there's nothing more naturally fulfilling than creating new lives, nurturing and giving them the gift of adventurous living. And be sure to tell them that when they grow old, there's no substitute for filling the gap of loneliness than the companionship of children and grandchildren.

Checkpoint Number Five: Do community work. Tell them that life is not complete without helping others and that civilization crumbles when people stop helping people. And you might add that when the family crumbles, civilization crumbles.

Checkpoint Number Six: Your teenagers are not too young to listen to what you know about New Thinking. Talk to them about it. This might stimulate them to investigate it further.

Everyman

Your advice will not only help my children, it will also help me. Your analogy that life, like a business venture, must be planned meticulously, struck a responsive chord in me. I didn't plan my life the way you described helping my children. When I convey your advice to them, some of it will rub off on me. But right now I'm worried about Checkpoint Number One, how to help my children direct their sexual drives in the present promiscuous sexual environment. Would you describe in your insightful way what's going on today so I can tell it to my children in a way that it will attract their attention?

Sage

Tell them what they probably vaguely know, that during the past fifty years the discipline of religious morality waned, and that they are caught in the net of popular promiscuity. Warn them against the loss of romance when there's nothing to hold back a young man, who, seeing a lithe body and an interesting conversationalist, nips a potential romance in the bud, when in a matter of hours or days he indulges in promiscuous sex and abruptly ends what could develop into a beautiful relationship. He smothers the bud of courtship and enduring love. Tell your children there's more excitement in a romantic touch than in a promiscuous clutch.

Everyman

How does the New Thinking address this issue?

Chapter Thirteen

Sage

New Thinking mores are closer to what they were fifty years ago than what they are now. In addition to physical attraction each partner should feel a strong hint that the other is more interested in "what I can do for you" than in "what you can do for me," something we discussed earlier. After the engagement, the ultimate ideal is to wait, excitedly, yes, until the marriage vows are exchanged before engaging in sexual intercourse. But if the desire is too great, let the honorable exception rejoice in mutual enjoyment. Spiritual pioneers are not stuck-in-the-mud nerds. We enjoy conviviality, fun and humor, with the extra adventure of living on the cutting edge of new ideas and diversity.

Everyman

Let's turn to a big, big world problem. Is there a correlation between our wounding the Earth and the Earth's wounding us?

Sage

Yes, the more we pollute the air, earth and water, the more nature will strike back with global warming, disease and natural calamities. The Earth is a living entity, and it will take the necessary action to heal its wounds. It is warning us, in no uncertain ways, that we had better heed its signs of protest and take action if we are to avert the looming natural catastrophes. The Earth has more resources to subdue us than we have to subdue it. We must come to the realization that the Earth can get along without us, but we can't survive without its life-giving resources. If we don't stop wounding each other, we may self-destruct back into primeval times or even extinction.

Everyman

You've posed the problem exceedingly well, but what's your solution?

Sage

There is only one long-range solution in the war between mankind and the Earth. That is to create new generations of spiritual scientists who, with the knowledge of the Fourth R schooling, will be prepared to heal the lacerations the mechanistic technologists have wrought. The scientific knowledge to reverse the ravaging encroachments of the Earth is already available, and more is on the way. All that's lacking is to graduate more new universalist Fourth R scientists to reinstate and nurture a healthy relationship between man and the Earth. The future spiritual scientists will structure, with God's guidance, a prudent partnership between meeting man's material needs and renewing the Earth's largess for our survival.

Everyman

I noticed that you included the phrase, "with God's guidance," in connection with the spiritual scientists constructing a plan to heal the Earth's wounds. Your interest in God's guidance is so central to your thinking that it's spilling over on me. Will you describe in detail exactly what goes on during your God-guidance meditation?

Sage

I'll begin with what happens when I sit down for my meditative sessions to seek God's guidance. I take about ten deep breaths to get the extra energy to keep my mind alert. Then I listen to my in-and-out breathing as I inaudibly repeat my mantra to clear my mind of intruding thoughts. But after a while, mundane thoughts begin to creep in anyway. I don't fight them. I remain relaxed, listening to my breathing. Some mornings nothing happens, except I get up from my chair with a relaxed body. At other times, an insight may pop into my mind to perk me up. Then relaxation changes to concentration. Many of my answers to your questions are the "hot" thoughts which made me get up from my chair. I jot them down so I won't forget them. When I'm through with my quiet time, I take another few minutes to consider any unusual thoughts, examining them in greater detail. Some thoughts may remain in my mind for several days, or even a week, as I evaluate them. When I'm convinced that a thought has merit, I adopt it as a new insight.

I view my meditation as a continuing education in the school of wisdom. I'm convinced that the Teacher, Cosmic Energy or God, is aware of my efforts to seek guidance, and my response is in the form of thoughts that excite my imagination. It's where my spiritual evolution accelerates. It's the Fourth R in action. It's where I go to church every morning, a church that has a membership of one.

Everyman

Thank you for sharing your personal experiences. You don't preach, you teach. I appreciate the difference. How about using the same, intimate experiences to show how New Thinking has benefited you physically, mentally, socially and commercially?

Sage

I've enjoyed benefits in each of these categories. The benefit I'm most grateful for is my new knowledge about the importance of proper breathing. Thoughtful, correct breathing has amazing healing power. Relying on my New Thinking insight, that breath is spiritual Cosmic Energy, I use it to heal my minor aches and pains. When a kink in my back, a rasp in my throat or a pain in my abdomen gets my attention, I mentally direct deep breathing to the complaining part of my body. I use this technique several times a day in three-to-five minute intervals. In a few days, the kinks, aches or pains subside, and most of the time fade away. I don't offer this method to anyone as a medical panacea, but for me it's an effective healing remedy. I assume that the extra oxygen directed to the ailing area helps the physical healing. Closely related to this physical healing is the mental benefit. When a cosmic-energy flow is impeded by anger, anxiety, fear or other negative emotion, it eventually reveals itself in disease. Medical science attests to that fact. When a debilitating emotion occurs, I turn for help to my cosmic breathing, in which I have the utmost confidence. I tell myself, "Let go of negative emotions and let the cosmic healing flow unimpeded." I don't allow the negative obstruction to fester by dwelling on its poisonous thoughts. This self-healing approach is an insight that originated during meditation and I've been nurturing and practicing it for years. After each of these minor healings I offer a thought of gratitude to my Cosmic Energy God. During my 85 years I've never been in a hospital for any ailment or operation. Remember this: Paying attention and communicating with your physical, mental and spiritual cosmic energies, minutes a day, is a healing prescription for a healthy life.

Everyman

What are some other benefits of your daily meditation?

Sage

I've changed from the carnivorous diet I followed when I was in a traditional religion to herbivorous foods which I was drawn to when I began to delve into New Thinking. This new diet has greatly improved my health. Animals are our less-evolved neighbors with whom we should share the Earth, not whom we should torture and kill for our food pleasure. Treating animals with compassion is a higher level of morality than sacrificing them for religious ceremonies or for hunting or eating pleasure. There are also economic reasons to abstain from carnivorous diets. It takes about thirty-five pounds of grain and hundreds of gallons of water to put one pound of meat on the table. And the most compelling reason for changing to a fruit/vegetable diet is that they are clean foods, while dead carcasses, no matter how appetizingly prepared, are toxic and deleterious to our health. For exercise, I walk three to four miles a day. I've done that for the past fifty years. That's about equivalent to walking twice around the Earth!

Everyman

New Thinking has certainly benefited you spiritually, and it's obvious it has benefited you physically and mentally. Tell me how you have benefited socially and commercially?

Sage

The kind of relationships we develop within our families and with our friends, including business associates and strangers, determines the degree of joy or misery we experience in our daily lives.

Here are a few examples I have tested in action and found rewarding in building social relations.

The most important of all is helping people in whatever ways we can. The mutual benefits this brings in goodwill and joy are immense! Also, I don't ever condemn anyone. When I'm tempted to do so, I remember that when I point a finger at my neighbor, I have three fingers pointing back at myself.

During a discussion in large groups, say, I prefer to contribute what I know to the group's welfare rather than finding something to disagree with.

In a one-to-one conversation, I concentrate more on what interests him or her rather than what interests me.

I avoid trying to win arguments, wanting to be right, because when I win, I usually lose a friend.

A sarcastic comment, no matter how tempted I am to say it, never passes my lips.

When I'm confronted with negative verbal abuse, I remain silent. I remember Jesus' teaching that meekness is not weakness, it's spiritual strength.

I view people's peculiarities, differences and beliefs with curiosity, never with diminishment. I don't compare people because I understand that each is unique.

These are not world-shaking insights, but they help cement friendly relationships. And I'm happy to say that I don't dislike anyone, and as far as I know, no one dislikes me.

Everyman

Tell me how New Thinking helps you in your business.

Sage

We plan the way you do, but with an extra dimension. The thirty members of our accounting and estate-planning firm practice spirituality in the workplace, a subject we discussed earlier. Each of us in the company works with the sense that a spiritual cosmic power is guiding us to be of service to people. We make this our main purpose in our workday and in our life. That's our uncodified religion. We don't attract sensational clients who make big waves and big money. Most of our clients are low-key, middle-class people who are not seized by an intense desire to strike it big. Neither are we. None of us is interested in one hundred thousand dollar cars or million-dollar mansions. We charge moderate fees and live moderate lifestyles. The area where we excel is in the joy and camaraderie within our group and among those we serve.

Business for me is not a grab bag for profit that excites, but a treasured feeling that fulfills. I can't resist the temptation here to swing from my personal experience to a general observation on what's happening within commercial globalization.

Bigness-power without caring for the welfare of people has collapsed empires. The British and Russian empires are recent examples of why bigness eventually fails when it's motivated primarily by acquisition and power. Dictators who were mesmerized by bigness eventually faced violence and death. The reason I'm citing these historical examples is that while commercial globalization is creating jobs, for which we should be grateful, business moguls and their giant corporations are falling into the same trap of their bigness-worshipping predecessors. Global commercial dictatorship will lead to violence in the future, just as all forms of dictatorships have led to violence in the past, engulfing the rich and the poor.

I've digressed too far, but only because I feel so strongly about this. Now, let's get back to what's on your mind.

Everyman

I don't mind your digressions. They make me think. But I prefer specific answers to futuristic observations. Many of my friends tell me I'm foolish to bother about New Thinking, when the most practical thing to rely on, they say, is just plain, practical common sense. What do you think about that? And what should I tell them?

Sage

I agree with your friends, but only to a point. Common sense is extremely valuable in solving secular problems. But we need transcendent wisdom to give meaning to what common sense is telling us. It's like using only our left brain without the right brain's guidance. We're awash with secular common sense but because we're willing to settle just for that, we find less meaning in our lives. Tell your friends that there is another world beyond common sense waiting to be explored. For instance, common sense will not illume the meaninglessness of bloated egos driven to amass huge fortunes that can't possibly be used in one lifetime. Can common sense stop a Hitler, a Stalin or a Pol Pot — or a crooked businessman?

Everyman

Convincing stuff but I doubt if I could convince any of my friends. Can we turn once again to this: Why am I enamored with the idea that uncertainties are filled with possibilities? Most of my friends think I'm nuts to prefer uncertainty over certainty in my real estate developments.

Sage

There would be no evolutionary progress without uncertainty. Consider yourself blessed with the gift for probing uncertainties. It's at the cutting edge of discovering new lands, creating all our material marvels and understanding who or what God is. Without probing, we'd still be barbarians. Uncertainty is the oxygen of creativity. Or to put it another way, the search for the Unknown is spiritual evolution at its finest.

Everyman

Why am I more exhilarated while I'm climbing than arriving, more quickened by creation than by possession?

Sage

Because, my uncertainty-loving friend, when we create, whether we're aware of it or not, we're in tune with the process of universal creation: God in action. We're in partnership with cosmic creation. Possession provides secular security, yes, but when it becomes its ultimate goal, it's stultification.

Everyman

You mean, I stop evolving when my main goal is owning real estate?

Sage

If everything else is secondary to possession, the answer is yes. Perhaps I'm too harsh, but a person who settles for possession without exploring spiritual wisdom is an ethical humanist at best, and a barren, rich man at worst.

Everyman

Closely related to my flirtation with creative uncertainties is my tendency to hurry, to rush time. I suppose my subliminal reason for it is that time is money, that time has to be productive. Anything wrong with being in a hurry to obtain results?

Sage

Take a cue from nature. It is evolving with majestic slowness. Waltzing is more beautiful than fox-trotting. A poised, serene woman is more attractive than a hurrying one. Time is to be savored and enjoyed, not frittered away in a quick fix, a quick buck, a quick gratification, or a quick anything. A life paced with poise is more gratifying, more orderly, more productive.

Everyman

Can you explain why despite my having been weaned from my orthodox religion, part of me still clings to my holy past? When I stood at the Wailing Wall in Jerusalem and put my hands on a piece of its venerable rock, goose pimples raced through my body. When I listen to the Hebrew song, "Aile, aile, lomo asaftoni," ("God, God, Why Have You Forsaken Us?"), during Yom Kippur temple services, my mind empties of everything except the holy words and the melancholy melody. This hallowed feeling is deeply imbedded in my psyche, just as Christian and Islamic yearnings for holiness are burned into their followers. Is it in the world's best interest to give up these precious, reverential joys, or is there a way to hold on to these feelings without having them lead us into religious wars?

Sage

The killings that have been going on between the Arabs and Israelis and elsewhere, are mainly the result of the hallowed feelings you describe. I understand them because I'm still enchanted with my Catholic traditions in the same way. They nourish me, as yours nourish you. And I respect the millions, of all religions, who still cherish theirs. New Thinking does not expect that traditionalists will give up their sacred emotions, only that they not use them as weapons against others. My solution is to keep one foot in tradition, and to use the other to explore the new wisdom of Universal Spirituality.

Everyman

I'm not convinced that the two can work together!

Sage

Let me cite an example that may convince you.

Everyman

As always, I'm eager to learn. I'm mindful that you are the teacher and I'm the student.

Sage

Well, I'd rather view us as students learning from each other. Here is an insight that I received from observing nature, the ultimate wisdom. Fusing traditional wisdom with New Thinking creates a wisdom that is greater than the sum of the two. Biologists confirm this principle with the analogy that when two cells unite, they form a new cell that is superior to each of the combined cells. It's a proven evolutionary principle. Is it not logical then to extrapolate that when traditional wisdom and New Thinking combine, they enrich each other to create a higher form of spiritual thinking that is different and superior to either one? What's true in nature, we can assume, is also true on the human scale. As above, so below. I'll be specific. I attended a symposium on humanistic studies at the Aspen Institute where the liberal Supreme Court Justice William Brennan was the moderator. He had just attended mass at a local church. I happened to be nearby. He put his arm around my shoulder to express his exuberance and said, "Isn't life wonderful!" That evening, at the old Aspen Opera House, which was filled to capacity, he delivered a lecture on liberal social compassion. The lecture was beamed to the seminar participants as well as to the local people. It combined the best of his religious wisdom with the best of New Thinking Universal Spirituality. He fused the wisdom of the Catholic cell with the wisdom of the New Thinking cell in a way that inspired an audience where there were many other religious cells. So you see, old-time religion and New Thinking can unite to form the best of both.

Everyman

Does the same two-cell analogy hold when we change from one religion to another? Does one cell die in the process?

Chapter Fourteen

Sage

Changing one set of traditions for another involves rejection instead of fusion, devolution instead of evolution. I know several people who changed religions. They accepted the new wisdom, but blocked out the old. There was no fusion. The cells didn't merge to create a new cell that was superior to either of the two.

I know a New-Thinking woman whose personal experiences in changing from one religion to another illustrate clearly why the cells collided instead of uniting. She grew up in a small town and reluctantly practiced her Catholic faith until she was twenty. Here is her story: "I didn't like to kiss the Bishop's ring when he came to town or submit to the many stifling rules. I changed to Lutheranism in the hope of finding something new to inspire my flagging interest in God. They preached the same do's and don'ts about virtue, love and responsibility, just as the Catholics did, but with greater emphasis on how to avoid the devil. That part of the liturgy was chilling to me, but I remained a Lutheran for several years because I enjoyed the camaraderie of singing in the chorus. At thirty-three, I got a job in Chicago and without any regrets, I left Lutheranism and joyfully joined Jehovah's Witnesses. The parishioners were exceedingly friendly and caring, and for a year I witnessed, from door-to-door, in my spare time. I truly enjoyed the fellowship but they demanded a price, that I follow a long list of prescribed don'ts that were more stringent and stranger than in my previous religions: not to salute the American flag; not to date outside Jehovah's Witnesses; not to celebrate Christmas or any birthdays; not to use blood transfusions and a dozen other don'ts. And if I didn't follow them, I would be disfellowshipped. I loved the people but not their rules.

Thirty years ago this holy rebel found her spiritual niche in New Universal Thinking and this is how she described her change, "Until I encountered New Thinking, I was a dissatisfied rebel, blaming one religion after another because each religion's wisdom demanded a regimen of rules I didn't like. But when I grasped the wisdom of spiritual evolution and Universal Spirituality, I changed from imposed discipline to self-discipline, from ritualizing a remote God to seeking God's intimate guidance in the privacy of my home. I changed from fragmented religious gods to One Universal God. In the light of my new understanding, instead of blame I have a new appreciation and respect for people who are building virtue by joyfully embracing the rules and rituals to guide them to their God. From the standpoint of spiritual evolution, their next evolutionary step will be to fuse their religious spiritual wisdom with Universal Spiritual wisdom, and blame each other no more. We'll have evolved to the illuminating understanding that it's as vital for religions to get along with one another as it is to heed the immortal Universal ideal to love one another.

Everyman

The woman you cite sounds like you. Do all New Thinkers follow a particular wisdom, as in the Bible?

Sage

Groups of people in many countries are penetrating and deepening the Universal Wisdom by studying, attending lectures and reading the new spiritual literature that has accelerated tremendously during the past ten years. The reason for this burst of interest is that whenever there's a dire need for change in human devolution, spiritual evolution comes to the rescue with new spiritual ideals, just as it previously formed new religions to meet new human needs.

Everyman

I want to get back for a moment to your intriguing analogy of the fusion of cells. Please tell me what happens to millions of unattached "cells," those who've fallen out of religion and those who've never been in religion. Just what and whom do they have to fuse with? Is it New Thinking?

Sage

There are three main groups of these unattached "cells." The first group consists of ethical humanists, atheists and, with some exceptions, wealthy secularists. The second is composed of disenchanted former religionists. The third group consists mostly of those who haven't found anything better to live for than coarsening our culture, trampling on our freedoms, creating social hubris and soiling the fabric of civilized life. Unfortunately, we're going to get little help from this first group of humanists, atheists and wealthy secularists because most of them are self-centered, self-assured and self-sufficient. The second group, which consists of one-time disenchanted religionists, are more responsive and constitute the main source of new apostles for New Thinking. I'm one of them.

The third group is our main challenge and opportunity, not only to reclaim "lost" lives, but also to help their evolution. Destructive "cells" will continue to destroy healthy "cells," until they are challenged with New Thinking, the way the heathens were challenged with the

Kingdom of God. Spiritual evolution has shown that it's possible for the worst of "cells" to fuse with the best of "cells" to form civilized cells for their mutual enlightenment. The early Christians did it; we can we can do it, too.

Everyman

What would you say if you were invited to speak before groups of gang members, casino owners, gun lovers, entertainment moguls and others of their ilk? They are our modern barbarians, the main cause of our cultural decay. What could you possibly say that could fuse their destructive "cells" with the New Thinking "cells?"

Sage

To gang members, I'd apologize for the shameful way our government has neglected them. Most of them have had no caring homes, no parental guidance, no family togetherness. So the gangs became their homes, their togetherness. It's human nature to want to belong, and I'd show them how they can "belong" to all society instead of just an isolated gang. The first thing is to take charge of their own life, as some ex-gang members have done, and become a part of all society. The first, the most important, step when starting a new life is to find work to fill empty hours. There are plenty of social agencies to help. I know former gang members who are now gardeners, painters, construction workers, and so on. Work is the greatest, the best therapy. It normalizes your life. So I'd advise them to take two steps. First, take personal charge of their life, and second, find work, any kind of work. Then set out on the uplifting adventure of creating a new life. You'll be amazed at the wonderful possibilities waiting for you. Just make up your mind to try the new, and I assure you that you'll never go back to the old! To casino owners, I'd say: You've been more creative in merchandizing gambling than religions have been in merchandizing morality. You've done it with such subtlety and respectability that even the government, which used to jail gamblers some fifty years ago, has been mesmerized by your success. It has joined with you in extricating hundreds of billions of dollars in lotteries, mostly from the pockets of the poor and middle class. Even some churches have succumbed to your scheme of giving gambling an aura of respectability, as in allowing bingo games in their houses of worship.

You are smart, intelligent and superb merchandisers. But you're not wise when it comes to putting the treasures of money ahead of the treasures of the spirit.

Metaphorically speaking, you're living in caves gilded with the glitter of luxury but sadly shut off from the outside light where much nobler life-fulfillments abound. It's the sunshine world of giving and helping, instead of the dark world of getting and hurting. What good is immense wealth when you can look back, at the end of your life, only on piles of money that you can no longer use, money that, in many instances, contributed to the breakup of homes and ruined countless lives? Come out into the sunshine! The world needs your skills to shore us up, not to slide us into another Sodom and Gomorrah.

To gun lovers, I'd say: When millions of people love guns more than they do lives, tragic consequences are inevitable. More people are killed by guns than die of drug abuse. You and you alone can dislodge this death embrace. Most of you are members of the NRA, the National Rifle Association, and most of you are good, God-believing people. But if you sincerely love God, you can be the ones to lead the crusade for a truly gunless society. You have the power to save hundreds of thousands of lives. In comparison, you'd be giving up so little for so much! Try to seek God's guidance in the privacy of your homes regarding what's best for our country, and then let God decide what's right instead of listening to your human self-interest.

Everyman

Persuasive advice, but the casino moguls who love money more than respectability and responsibility, along with the NRA who prize guns ahead of lives, will not budge from what fulfills them.

Sage

You're right. We can write them off. But their great, great-grandchildren and beyond, schooled in the wisdom of the

Fourth R, will look back on their ancestors as myopic men who fed their lives with shallow excitement, and starved their souls of spiritual treasures.

To entertainment moguls, I'd say: With few exceptions, you are long on creativity but short on elevating human nature. During the last fifty years, low-level creativity has inundated our culture with coarse art, music, literature and sensational entertainment. The good and the sublime were also there, but in a whisper compared to the roar of the vulgar and mediocre. I say to you creative artists: Don't stunt the growth of your imperishable souls for perishable loot and fame. It's a lose/lose deal. It diminishes you and your creativity. I appeal to you who have been blessed with the gift of creativity that you listen to your inner voice where the gift of true creativity abides; don't pander to the popular and succumb to diminishing yourself and society.

Everyman

As a finale to our conversation I'd like to make this proposition: You've offered at least a dozen ideas that are new to me and most people. To sum up, I'd like you not only to reclarify them one-by-one, but also to defend their worldwide spiritual benefits. I'm going to play the devil's advocate.

Sage

Go ahead! I'm ready.

Chapter Fifteen

Everyman

Number One: Wholeness. You made such a big deal about being One with the Universe and how that feeling brings us closer together and more in sync with all the entities within the Universe. How can the idea of Wholeness make me feel one with poison ivy, a ferocious tiger, a killer in Afghanistan? You're asking me to fly when I can't crawl. I don't find any value in Wholeness because it's so remote from my physical, emotional and mental needs. It's a pale promise to my personal welfare compared to the promise of a personal God who endows me with everlasting life, providing I lead a virtuous existence. So tell me why I should become interested in Wholeness? What personal benefit does it offer?

Sage

Wholeness will not put money in the bank or assure your

personal salvation. But if you stop to think, not for a few fleeting moments but for a relaxed period of time, you'll come to realize that everything within the Universe is interrelated and interconnected in an orderly, unified way. If not, everything in the Universe would fly apart and disintegrate. Just as the organs of our bodies depend upon one another for their mutual existence, so all the entities within the Universe — its organs — are interwoven into a wholeness for their mutual protection. The more we understand and feel the truth of this universal fact, the more we'll see the folly of fragmentation, as compared to the benefits of cooperation. The world's concern with ecology, the environment, global warming and so on, is really the slow awakening to the stupendous importance of understanding the concept of Wholeness. When we do, we'll know why universal Wholeness is more spiritual than particularized religious Holiness. Accepting the concept of Wholeness helps us to understand and appreciate the role of diversity. Wholeness, in short, is wisdom. With it we see more, comprehend more, enjoy more.

Everyman

Number Two: Evolution. It's not as appealing as the Kingdom of God. Wouldn't you agree that most people are far more interested in heaven than in how they evolved? Why should we give up our trust in a personal God, who has sustained mankind for centuries, and rely on evolution, which promises nothing more than that it is a scientific fact? There are many scientific facts out there, but they are too remote to intimately engage our lives. Personal religions, with all their faults and limitations, have civilized us. What can evolution offer that is equally beneficial? Why should we switch from a personal God, who has done so much for us, to the concept of an evolutionary, scientific God? Tell me why I should be inspired more by evolution than by religious wisdom, which has endured and sustained us for centuries.

Sage

Scientific evolution has thrust us into a new way of looking at our human progress. Creational religions have evolved us out of heathenism, but now a new phase of spiritual evolution is challenging us to advance beyond creationism. New Thinking is following in the footsteps of the brave scientists who, centuries ago, challenged religion to change its belief that the sun revolved around the Earth. With physical evolution generally accepted as a fact, we can no longer plan our destinies on the basis of past religious assumptions. Instead, we must explore how we can enrich our lives using the new spiritual wisdom, such as reincarnation, which promises an eternity of physical lives instead of one life in perpetuity in heaven. For me evolution is not just a pedantic theory but a vibrant conviction that has vitalized and propelled my spiritual evolution. It's as much a future Kingdom of God for me as heaven is for the most devout creationists.

Everyman

Number Three: Spiritual evolution. I never heard of this until you explained that the main reason for the world's human depravity and misery is that spiritual evolution is only 5,000 years old compared to physical evolution, which is millions of years old. You claim that spiritual evolution is a profound wisdom to which religions have paid no attention, as a consequence of which they are still clinging to old-time religious beliefs to alleviate human misery. I find your insight convincing but also baffling. Why do most of us still act like savages when a few seem to be almost saints? Why, after 5,000 years of spiritual evolution, have Hitler's hordes burned innocent men, women and children in crematoriums, and others have risked their lives to help people in many dangerous places on Earth? Why did the bad people evolve equally alongside the good? You told me there's justice in nature, then why have the savages evolved alongside the saints? What's your explanation?

Sage

The new wisdom of spiritual evolution puts the spotlight on the main reason that there's so much human misery in the world. There are two basic explanations of why we have less-evolved and more-evolved people. First, there are young souls and older souls. Not all human souls were formed and began evolving at the same time, so that the older ones have had many more incarnations than have the younger ones. And second, we can logically surmise that some humans made greater efforts to evolve than did others. You and I can see it clearly in our midst. So, during the last 5,000 years, the older souls — who, in addition, made greater evolutionary effort than the younger souls who made little effort — also attained greater strides in spiritual development, especially those within religions. The younger souls who made little effort to evolve are creating most of the havoc on Earth. This is a quick but basic answer to those who are perplexed about why there are savages and saints living side by side on planet Earth.

Everyman

Number Four: Periodicity. New Thinking will make little headway with periodicity. It's a cold, complicated word that doesn't arouse any warm response, like compassion, kindness or forgiveness. Yet you tout it as one of the cardinal principles of New Thinking. What is its attraction? Why should I take the time to explore its meaning?

Sage

I admit that periodicity is a conversation-stopper, but if we take the time to explore its meaning, we'll be rewarded with a clear explanation of the evolutionary role it plays in the Universe. Cosmic creation uses periodicity to create new forms through the process of generation, degeneration and regeneration. The march of creation, the process of constant becoming does not evolve in a straight line, but through periods of change, cycles, new beginnings and old endings. Because of the myriad, different compositions of all the universal entities, some cycles last hours, days, years and millennia. The Earth, for instance, is 4.5 billion years old, and according to scientists, it will change into a new composition 4.5 billion years hence. Yes, periodicity explains how universal process works, including our human cyclical role of reincarnation.

Everyman

Number Five: Reincarnation. You've done a convincing job of explaining why we should believe in reincarnation, but I still have some doubts. For instance, does a seed of a flower have a soul that remembers its life in a previous flower, or a calf a soul that remembers its life as a cow? Because we're a more evolved animal, should that give us the chutzpah to believe that our soul remembers its past life, but that the plants and animals don't? If it is not likely that the seed and calf remember, why should we assume that we do, in the form of inherited capacities, as you so convincingly explained? I may be naïve in raising this objection, but I'm trying to remove my lingering doubts because reincarnation has gripped my imagination.

Sage

Your logical mind is working well. Your question about what roles the seed and the calf play in the process of reincarnation gives me a chance to refer to what I've read by seers regarding the difference between group souls of minerals, plants and animals, and individualized souls of man. The soul energy sustains the lower-evolved forms by means of a group soul for each category. As the mineral evolves into the plant, and the plant into the animal, the group soul evolves also from the mineral to the plant to the animal. Then, the intuitive seers claim, from among the most evolved animals, a few will split off from the group soul and evolve into primitive man with an individualized but primordial soul. These Homo Sapiens evolved into Neanderthal, then Cro-Magnon then into the civilized men and women we are today. Our individualized souls not only remember the capacities that we inherit from previous lives, but some of us, as Dr. Ian Stevenson pointed out in his book I mentioned earlier, remember the actual details of our past lives. And as our souls take greater charge of our lives, the few will become the many who will remember in greater detail our experiences of past lives.

Everyman

Number Six: The role of the soul. There is no greater division between traditional and New Thinking than in the role of the soul. The traditionalists put their ultimate belief in the permanency of the body, whereas New Thinking puts its ultimate faith in the permanency of the soul, the eternal part of us that uses transitory bodies to refine physical experience into spiritual wisdom. That, roughly, is your explanation. If that's true, then the difference is unbridgeable. The traditionalists would have to negate their ultimate belief in physical salvation in order to agree to the subordination of the body to the soul. And New Thinking would have to give up its belief in reincarnation to agree in the permanency of the body. How are you going to overcome this colossal difference? How can this new version of the role of the soul be accepted when arrayed against it are centuries-old cherished beliefs, the very foundation of religious wisdom? It's an irreconcilable difference.

Sage

Traditional religions believe that the soul is the most spiritualized part of the body. New Thinking believes that the soul energy is not only the most spiritualized part of the body, it is also the only permanent part of the body. It is the soul that evolves spiritually, not the body. The body dies; the soul lives on. It is the soul that leads us to eternity, not the body.

Religious desire for personal bodily salvation has served mankind exceedingly well, and still does. New Thinking is not negating its verity, nor its ability to inspire, discipline and build virtue. New Thinking is introducing a new role for the soul, which in its view also has validity. An increasing number of people are finding a new inspirational road to eternity. Spiritual evolution will play the role of letting mankind choose between the two versions of the soul. The New Thinkers will do it amiably, because it's at the core of their open-ended idealism. We hope the traditionalists will defend their beliefs just as amicably. Time and the truer version will determine the outcome.

Chapter Sixteen

Everyman

Number Seven: Universal Spirituality. Since each religion proclaims its own universal spirituality for mankind, it will spurn New Thinking's Universal Spirituality as nothing more than what it is already offering. Religions have successfully warded off all attempts to change their faiths by branding as false those who tried to do so. They regard your New Thinking as just another cult. This criticism has worked in the past, and they're confident it'll work now and always. Might not Universal Spirituality, one of your cardinal principles, turn out to be, as they say, a "false god?"

Sage

One hundred years ago, Universal Spirituality was regarded as one of those ephemeral new religious ideas that come and go, but today millions are believing that the idea of Universal Spirituality is leading us back to the original concept of One Universal God. Seekers of new spiritual wisdom, and to some extent traditionalists, are beginning to see the colossal mistake religious leaders made — when after many gods evolved into One God, they fragmented the One God idea back to many religious Gods. To their discredit, they were more interested in who was right regarding God than in what was right. This blunder cost millions of lives, and the tragic divisions are still with us. At stake is the continuation of religious strife or the peaceful sharing of new universal spiritual wisdom.

Everyman

Number Eight: The first duality, devolution and evolution. When we were discussing what came first, matter or spirit, I wondered about how it would benefit the average person to know this. And when you explained that evolution/devotion was the primal duality out of which all other dualities flow, I was convinced that all this esoteric stuff had nothing to do with what my life is all about. If New Thinkers are going to rely on this kind of information to attract adherents, my common sense tells me that they're not going to get very far. It's okay for pundits to fool around with this arcane stuff, but not for guys whose main interest is to make a living, or for entrepreneurs whose main priority is to make a profit.

Sage

The most direct, clear reason why you should be interested in devotion/evolution is that unless we unreservedly believe that the Universe evolved out of Spirit, out of which everything flows, rather than out of unguided, chaotic muck, we deny the existence of God. For New Thinking there is no ambiguity: Spirit, God all came first. And the primal duality helps us to catch a glimpse of why Spirit descends devolutionarily into matter. It is to creatively express Itself, using devolution to descend into matter, and evolution to evolve matter back to its Originating Source. That's how God, the creative process, works. The difference between the mechanistic scientists, who deny God, and the spiritual scientists, who believe that matter came out of Spirit, gives added scientific credence to the existence of God. The devolution/evolution assumption is not some arcane theory but a practical supposition out of which flows a firm belief in God. Without this supposition it's easy to slide into atheism and become mechanistic automatons roaming the Earth.

Everyman

Number Nine: Seeking God's guidance during quiet time. When I tried meditating some years ago, after I read an article on its value, my mind was filled with thoughts about what I had said to people, what they had said to me, along with a lot of inconsequential mishmash that kept circulating in my mind. I couldn't shut it off. After fifteen minutes of restlessly sitting in my chair, I got up more tense than relaxed. I tried meditating several times with the same result. Most people I know don't pay any attention to meditation, and the few I know who have tried it experienced failures similar to mine. Traditional religionists prefer sermons, hymns and ceremony over seeking God's guidance in the privacy of their homes.

If most religious people don't seek daily guidance, how can you expect millions who are not involved in organized religion to practice as difficult a discipline as only a handful of sages have mastered? Might not this idea of God's guidance also prove to be one of those "fallen gods?" I like what it's done for you, but aren't you asking the impossible of the masses?

Sage

Moses' Ten Commandments civilized the Israelites, Jesus' Kingdom of God converted the Romans and Mohammed's Koran disciplined the Moslems. They asked for the impossible; their difficulties were enormous. Seeking God's guidance is as new and formidable an ideal to put into practice for our times, as the resistances were for their times. Moral Re-Armament is changing the human nature of tens of thousands with its emphasis on seeking God's guidance during a daily hour of meditation. Its practice has changed the lives of crooked labor leaders, go-go girls, terrorists, slimy politicians and others with impossible-to-change natures, in and out of religion.

Religious wisdom is holding back the torrent of malevolence, for which we should be grateful, but its rite and rote are not powerful enough to stop it. A daily and intimate communication with God has a far better chance to elevate our human nature individually, and eventually collectively. Our challenge is to create new spiritual inspirational literature and massive grassroots discussion to show how we can find God in a new, more rewarding way. It will take a long time, but just imagine the kind of civilization we would have if most people would take personal charge in seeking God's guidance rather than having the clergy digesting it for them. This change is possible. It will occur. Perhaps you and I will meet in a future incarnation to enjoy the coming enlightened age in which seeking God's guidance during meditation is the norm rather than the exception.

Everyman

Number Ten: Cosmic energy God. I've tried to keep an open mind but I can't warm up to your concept of a cosmic energy God. And I can safely assume that more people would regard it with skepticism at best, and ridicule it at worst. Contemplating God in man's image draws us closer to what we're familiar with, while imagining God as

Cosmic Energy distances God into a remote abstraction. Why should people change from a warm, personal God to a cold energy God? The vast majority of people who are not privy to your knowledge will shrug it off as not worthy of attention. Of all your New Thinking ideas, this one, in my view, is the least acceptable.

Sage

Spiritual scientists are exploring new ideas to benefit our age in the way the prophets explored new values for their age. Using Einstein's cosmic science, where they find the noblest version of God, they add Cosmic Energy to the other designations — Spirit, Divine Mind, Universal Consciousness, as well as other versions. The new designation defines God as Cosmic Energy because it is the only entity that is ubiquitous, all-inclusive, all in all. Nothing exists outside of Cosmic Energy, or outside of God. It is total, as is God. And this spiritual Cosmic Energy has intention, purpose and cosmic super-intelligence to guide everything in the Universe.

When I breathe, think, walk or talk, it is Cosmic Energy that is sustaining and renewing me with a speck of its Cosmic Energy, as it is doing for all entities in the Universe. When I seek God's guidance during my quiet time, God is there, as close as every thought and breath I take. There is nothing remote or abstract about my Cosmic Energy God. When an elevating thought enters my mind, I know it is my Cosmic Energy God communicating with me. Anyone who wants to make his or her life more interesting, more meaningful, more fulfilling, can experience it. You don't have to be a sage to comprehend it. All you need is the willpower to persist in overcoming the initial failures in seeking God's guidance. A Cosmic Energy God is closer to us than God visualized as being in faraway heaven. Both concepts refer to the same God. What's important is that we find the best way to listen to God's thoughts without the distractions that block God's "voice."

Everyman

Number Eleven: The Fourth R. If I understand you correctly, unless the Fourth R is accepted and taught in all public and religious schools, our self-destruction will continue unabated. If the guardians of the separation of church and state and traditional religions stop the teaching of the Fourth R, will New Thinking die on the vine? Might not New Thinkers share the same fate that has befallen mystics throughout history? Isn't it possible that mankind is not ready for New Thinking's Fourth R, not evolved enough to "move mountains?" I tend to agree with you that Universal Spirituality can save us but most people are not ready for this Fourth R. If it is a prerequisite to all other New Thinking ideas, then I remain a realist. Can you get me out of my pessimism and into your optimism?

Sage

You're a realist, but realism combined with pessimism will get us nowhere. We're at a juncture in history where civilization is in such disarray that pragmatic realism is not enough. We need the powerful, world-changing ideal that has always been on the mystical fringe, and we need to put it into the mainstream of everyday human affairs. What I mean is no less than articulating what the mystics always knew regarding the next step in spiritual evolution, to which religion paid little attention, keeping the multitudes completely ignorant. Today the educated are probing what might be generally referred to as new spiritual wisdom, and New Thinkers are valiantly trying to make this wisdom understandable to the masses.

For instance, twenty-five years ago a Catholic bartender who was smitten with New Thinking formed a five-member group of New Thought in Palm Springs, California. Today they have 1,800 members who meet twice a week to discuss the core wisdom of New Thinking. There are thousands of such enclaves, large and small, on five continents. There are practical mystics who are exploring what was hidden from the people for centuries. From among these new spiritual pioneers will arise the men and women of tomorrow who will articulate the essence of the Fourth R, something the mystics explored in the privacy of their homes.

There is no far-reaching alternative to halting our slide

into the abyss of a new dark age other than elevating our human nature on a mass scale via the teaching of universal spiritual wisdom from the first grade through college. I know this is not the practical benefit you are looking for now, but what is more practical than to feel that inspirational surge that our freedom fighters felt several hundred years ago when they fought for the freedoms you and I enjoy today? The good they did for us we can do now for future generations.

Everyman

Number Twelve: Making "helping one another" the main purpose of our life. Can we make helping people a global "religion" as you tried to convince me earlier? I don't think so. I admit it's easier than "loving one another." But is it realistic to believe that creationists would give it priority over personal salvation, or secularists put it ahead of their self-interests? This is as impossible as asking us to become angels. So tell me why we should change our priorities, and make helping people our prime purpose in life?

Sage

Obviously, elevating our human nature to make helping people a world cultural religion is not going to happen soon. But let me tell you why it will eventually happen. First, it's already happening. People are helping each other on a far greater scale than at any time in history.

The irony is that there is also more havoc in society and people are also killing each other in greater numbers than at any time in history. Again, let me tell you why the helping ideal will prevail.

As human misery increases, those who have too much will eventually evolve into asking, "What for?" They'll begin probing for something more, as you're doing now. New Thinking will provide the answer. And those who don't have enough will find that alleviation of their plight will be achieved only through nonviolence. Loving one another was asking too much, as religious wars have shown. But helping one another is more realistically doable, as evidenced by the fact that more and more people are finding that giving is more fulfilling than getting. Spiritual evolution is helping people discover the concept of Wholeness through the ideal of helping others. Its practice has the universal potential to usher in the Messianic Age for which millions are waiting. If optimism is the oxygen of human progress, then I've given you a strong whiff of it. Breathe it in — deeply!

Chapter Seventeen

Everyman

I held back on the most crucial question, one that involves our very lives, in our own country. I didn't want to get it mixed up with New Thinking because I feared it would dilute and confuse both. Now that we've ended a most illuminating discussion on New Thinking, I'm anxious to hear what you have to say about the war now raging against terrorism. We're locked in a conflict that we dare not lose, but we're at a loss how to win. What's going on is related to much of what we've been discussing, and I hope you can clear my confusion about its cause and, more important, offer a solution that's as persuasive as the answers to many of my New-Thinking questions.

Sage

You and I have read many thoughtful opinions about the

causes and solutions to this unprecedented war against fundamentalist terrorism. I'd like to add a New-Thinking dimension to clarify the causes and solution.

First the causes: Some are obvious, others bordering on the esoteric. These are some of the obvious ones: Nearly all Moslem nations are dictatorships and their religions are dictated by the clergy with very little freedom to question the Koran's literal certainties. This is in sharp contrast to democracies in which Christian religions have the freedom to question the literal scriptures, and in some cases reject them. That's why New Thinking acquired a foothold in democracies but was shut out in Moslem countries. That's why Allah is more deeply ingrained in their psyches than God is in the developed democracies. And that's why we have the Khomeinis, and bin Ladens who are fiercer in their devotion to the love of Allah than the Falwells and Robertsons, who are equally devoted to God, but have been liberalized by the freedoms of democracy to use moral suasion instead of violence.

Another related cause for terrorism is the war between the Moslem moderates and the extremists. Turkey and Jordan are leaning toward democracy, while Iran and Afghanistan reverted to theocracy. And the fundamentalist terrorists in Egypt and Algeria, Pakistan and the other Moslem countries are violently conspiring to emulate Iran and Afghanistan.

The triggering cause that ignites the fear and fury of

Moslems is that they fear that the moderates will defile Allah by emulating the democratic West's moral decadence generated by unbridled freedoms.

This brings me to the not-so-obvious causes for Moslem terrorism. Why is their love for Allah as great as their hate for those who oppose them? It's inherited in the Moslem's reincarnational past that a few among them are born with their former fury for violence. But eventually, they too will evolve into peaceful Moslems. This leads me to the most important part of your question: What's the solution?

Everyman

That's what I'm waiting for. Your causes for terrorism have been most revealing. I hope you can top them with an equally believable solution.

Sage

To have done nothing after the September 11th World Trade Center massacre would have been a poor solution. To bomb Afghanistan was a murky choice. It fulfilled Osama bin Laden's plan that the bombing of the World Trade Center would be followed by a retaliatory bombing, which would kill innocent Moslems and as a result enrage moderates to swell his ranks. As he must have hoped, the mini-conflict between democracy and theocracy has swelled into a full-blown world war. The potential dangers are greater than in World War I and World War II because the weapons are far deadlier. Unless the war is stopped soon, it could spread and annihilate hundreds of millions of people. Neither side can win. Both are sure to lose.

Now for the more important part of your question — the solution.

The New-Thinking solution is to call a World Conference and invite representatives of the leading Moslem fundamentalists (who may belong to terrorist groups), moderate Moslems (who are fighting the terrorist cells in their own countries), and leaders from democracies (like George Mitchell, Colin Powell and Tony Blair), to discuss for several weeks or longer what each needs, what each one wants from others, and then seek agreement on the absolutely only war-stopping wisdom, to live with each other's political, religious and cultural differences without imposing them on one another.

During the blaming and accusations, as well as the admissions of wrongs and callousness, it's possible that a whiff of spiritual evolution might break through above the din of old thinking and illumine the minds of the terrorists, with the cosmic wisdom that Allah might be pleased more with their living amicably alongside "infidels" than killing them and being killed, that moderates should look for ways to find common ground with the fundamentalists, and that the West would gain more by trying to understand rather than blame Moslems, and by helping them to raise their standards of living. All this new thinking could cast a new light on the war during the weeks of discussion.

Everyman

What are the chances of convening such a world conference?

Sage

Not good, but possible.

Everyman

And what are the chances of the terrorists losing their
fury to kill, or for the moderates to find common ground
with the fundamentalists, or for the West to try to understand the Moslems and help them to raise their standards
of living, if such a world conference should take place?

Sage

Very unlikely, but possible.

Everyman

So it's worth a try?

Sage

Yes. You must have noticed that throughout our discussion, I favored optimism or pessimism, the possible over
the impossible.

The terrorists' cancer will be healed only with New
Thinking, never with mindless violence. As naïve as the
World Conference to stop today's Armageddon may
sound, it will eventually have to start with New-Thinking
solutions. Let me cite an example why I'm optimistic.

After a thousand years of czarist dictatorship, Mikhail Gorbachev dared the impossible: he opened the door ever so slightly to democracy, Boris Yeltsin walked in, and Vladimir Putin institutionalized it. That was a greater evolutionary impossibility than convening a World Conference, a meeting that is desperately needed, one whose success is so crucial. If ignored, the war will spread its cancerous growth and end civilization as we know it today.

Everyman

Your solution is too idealistic, and bin Laden is not about to become a Gorbachev. But I have to agree with your optimism. Just as uncertainties are full of opportunities, so impossibilities are open to opportunities.